MW00396896

STEEL HELMET
AND MORTARBOARD

LT. COL. C.R. COFFEY
COMMANDING
OUT

STEEL HELMET AND MORTARBOARD

An Academic in Uncle Sam's Army

FRANCIS H. HELLER

UNIVERSITY OF MISSOURI PRESS COLUMBIA AND LONDON

University of Missouri Press, Columbia, Missouri 65201
Printed and bound in the United States of America

5 4 3 2 1 13 12 11 10 09

Library of Congress Cataloging-in-Publication Data

Heller, Francis Howard.
Steel helmet and mortarboard : an academic in Uncle Sam's Army / Francis H. Heller.
p. cm.
Summary: "The story of an Austrian refugee who earned an American law degree in 1941, but a year later was drafted into the U.S. Army. Heller's account of those years recalls how he adjusted to military life and then how he later resumed his academic career only to be recalled to active duty for the Korean War"–Provided by publisher.
Includes index.
ISBN 978-0-8262-1838-4
1. Heller, Francis Howard. 2. World War, 1939-1945–Personal narratives, American. 3. World War, 1939-1945–Participation, Austrian American. 4. World War, 1939-1945–Pacific Area. 5. Soldiers–United States–Biography. 6. United States. Army–Military life–History–20th century. 7. Austrian Americans–Biography. 8. Refugees–United States–Biography. 9. World War, 1939-1945–Refugees. 10. Law teachers–Kansas–Lawrence–Biography. I. Title.
D811.H4419A3 2009
940.54'1273092–dc22
[B] 2009008542

™ This paper meets the requirements of the American National Standard for Permanence of Paper for Printed Library Materials, Z39.48, 1984.

Design and composition: Jennifer Cropp
Printer and binder: Thomson-Shore, Inc.
Typefaces: Minion and Caslon

Frontispiece: Staff of the 758th Field Artillery Battalion, Kansas Reserve, at Fort Bragg (l to r) Capt. F. H. Heller, Lt. Col. Cecil R. Coffey, Maj. W. O. Tainter, Capt. Jay R. Jennings, Capt. G. B. Moats.

CONTENTS

PREFACE

Dachau, about fifteen miles northwest of Munich, on a chilly day in late March 1946: Just about a year earlier, advance elements of the United States Army had reached this, Nazi Germany's oldest concentration camp. They found the camp abandoned by its guards but filled with inmates—some dead, the rest in horrifying states of malnourishment, disease, and physical deterioration. The inmates were now all gone. A part of the prison camp had since been cleaned and repaired; it held Germans convicted of war crimes who awaited transfer to their ultimate places of confinement. The Allies had not yet decided the future of the rest of the camp.

Four American officers, all in three-quarter-length khaki wool coats, were about to tour the unrestored parts of the facility. Only someone familiar with U.S. Army insignia would have recognized that the four came from the other side of the world: their shoulder patches indicated that they belonged to units on occupation duty in Japan. I was one—indeed the lowest-ranking—of the four. Later I'll detail the story of the army detachment whose assignment it was in early 1947 to escort roughly eleven hundred German nationals, mostly civilians, from the Far East to Germany. After our stop in Shanghai there were seventeen members of the German armed forces, in this group most of whom had been assigned to China to assist the Japanese high command there, mainly with the installation and operation of counterintelligence equipment that was to gather data about U.S. forces. When Germany surrendered on May 8, 1945, these men had carried on (i.e., they had continued to wage war after their government had agreed to cease belligerency). For this they had been tried and convicted by a military commission established by the United States and sitting in

Shanghai. They were to serve their sentences in prison facilities in Germany under American control. Our delivery of them to Dachau was the first step in Germany on their way to their place of confinement.

Our escort detail included about thirty military policemen. Given their choice, they opted, as one, to spend three days skiing. We four officers, all combat veterans of the war in the Pacific, chose to see some of the sights, starting with Dachau. The colonel in charge of the camp had warned us that there was not much to see; all the skeletal materials had been removed. Still the racklike boards that had served as beds, the piles of rotting prison garb, and the pervasive odor of decay assaulted the senses. My three cohorts gave voice to their horror.

I stayed behind and remained quiet. I could not help reflecting on the day in Vienna, give or take eight years earlier, when a friend from my school days, now wearing the brown shirt and swastika armband of a Nazi storm trooper, had come to me in the middle of the night to warn me that I faced arrest in just a few hours by the Gestapo, the feared secret police of the Hitler regime that, just a month earlier, had absorbed my native Austria. An active supporter of the former government, I knew that I was in jeopardy. Had it not been for my friend's nocturnal alert and my own knowledge of the river, which I eventually crossed under cover of darkness into neighboring Czechoslovakia, I would, in all likelihood, have met my end in Dachau or some similar place of terror.

Had my friend survived the war and the need and suffering of the postwar years? I would not see him again for almost thirty years. It was in 1965; my family and I had just finished dinner at his home in Vienna. He beckoned me into the living room; he had only a marginal knowledge of English, and my wife and son neither spoke nor understood German; he was as eager to learn about my life in the intervening years as I was to learn about his. I felt the urgent need to tell him of the emotions I had experienced that night in Dachau. To my surprise he denied that the visit to me had ever happened! I had the distinct feeling that he wished that I had not raised the subject.

As the years went by and I visited Vienna more frequently, we would always meet; he would drive us out into the Vienna Woods, where we would share wine and talk. The matter of his warning visit never came up again until the last time we saw each other, in 1997. By this time we were both eighty years old, and he had begged off the ride into the woods. We met at a small eating place in his neighborhood—what the Viennese call a Beisel. The proprietor evidently knew the neighborhood doctor; he did not wait for an order but immediately came and poured the wine for us. To my shock, my friend dropped his glass, looked at me with tears in his eyes, and uttered just one word, "Parkinson." The calamity had clearly occurred before; the innkeeper brought (and filled) another glass and placed a large napkin on my friend's lap. Turning to me, he explained in a gentle voice that after the many years the doctor had spent caring for the people in the district, it was only proper that they take care of him now.

My friend added that he had been given less than a year to live, and he was glad that we had one more, probably the last, opportunity, to talk. He said he had been living a lie. After every visit with me he had confessed to his wife that he had, once again, failed to confirm my recollection of that nocturnal warning. He had wanted to tell me how pleased he was that I had seemingly done well in America, but he had yielded to the continuing fear that if it became known that he had access to the Gestapo's arrest list in those early fear-dominated days of Nazi control, his denazification proceedings might be reopened and he could even lose his license to practice medicine. (Actually, in Austria these fears had become groundless only a few years after the end of the war.) Now these concerns no longer disturbed him; this was the last time we would meet and he could, without fear of consequences, let me know that he had taken great pride in my achievements and some consolation in the feeling that he had made it possible for me to become not just a professor but an American professor. After each of our meetings, he said, he had marveled at how much of an American I had become. How had that happened?

He was obviously relieved that we did not pursue the topic as we reminisced about our younger days. A year later he succumbed to his illness.

But the question he had raised stayed with me. Clearly I had turned into somebody different than I might otherwise have been. Quite apart from my friend's intervention, what influences had turned me into an American? (When, in 2004, the Austrian government awarded me its Cross of Honor for Science and Art, I accepted the distinction but not without some misgivings, for Austria had long ago ceased to be "home.")

It probably made a difference that I arrived in this country alone. Different from most new arrivals in the United States, I became totally immersed in an environment that discouraged retention, let alone renewal, of previously held cultural values.

The more I considered my past, the more important did my experience among enlisted soldiers in an American combat unit loom. It had transformed me physically and mentally and given me an understanding of life in the United States that I would not likely have attained if, for instance, I had trained and performed my military service, like young Henry Kissinger, as a translator and interpreter.

Over the years, various friends have urged me to put my recollections on paper. I felt I needed to do more than a narrative—that I should try to explain myself. Apart from occasional short-term jobs, I have had only two principal employers in my life: the United States Army and the University of Kansas. What difference did that make? And how did these ostensibly contrasting experiences affect each other?

I have never kept a diary; in later years an appointment calendar became a necessity, but it was never complete, and I never used it to record what a particular meeting or conference was about. Some of my friends would charge me with having a photographic memory; I do not think that is the case. I have a fairly good recall of things and events, and I have done considerable reading in books dealing with events I have participated in or been witness to; some of the readings may be reflected in my recollections. Occasionally in these pages I relate words spoken by others or by me; whenever this occurs, I do not pretend to be literal, but I am reasonably certain to reflect the sense of the language spoken. I have kept to a minimum the instances in which I have felt it appropriate to preserve a person's anonymity. In the case of Japanese names I have used Western practice (i.e., family name last). In another attempt at uniformity, I have consistently used the English Father in references to priests, although a speaker of German would use Pater, a Latin word.

The last chapter of this book bears the questioning caption "Serendipity or Good Fortune?" That alternative may have occurred to the reader throughout, possibly beginning with this preface. There are only a few footnotes, few of them reflecting research. All I relate are facts, events that have involved me.

Early versions of the manuscript I typed myself, but Robin Louise Miller, for about twenty years now the star of the staff in the dean's office at the University of Kansas Law School, can proudly claim to have done later versions—time and again. Others on the staff have assisted her, but she deserves the lion's share of my gratitude.

If my wife, Donna, had not been stricken late in 1989 with cancer and succumbed a year later, she would be listed—as she is on some of my other works. She was my most valued supporter and assistant.

As it is, there were persons who were briefly but crucially important in one or more of the stories I relate and others who affected me over a longer time but perhaps not so emphatically. I should like to list in chronological order some from both categories with brief explanations. I owe them all, but the list is exhaustive.

My stepmother, Denise, had to struggle with a youngster only seven teen her junior when she married my widowed father. We became friends in later years, and I hope I was able to tell her that with gratitude on my face.

The monks-teachers at my Benedictine school were, to a man, exemplars of exceptional levels of educational skill. I continue to acclaim how solid my pre-university schooling in Vienna was. Of my fellow students I have already mentioned Gustav Zahourek (later M.D.), but others could be named; I was not actually a very sociable type as a youngster.

Except for Zahourek's warning, I was unaided in my nightly crossing of the river between Austria and Czechoslovakia. My father, a resident since my sixteenth year in the capital of Poland, Warsaw, had paid for my travel on a Polish liner from Danzig (now Gdansk) to New York, and sent me with a check for two hundred U.S. dollars and twenty letters of recommendation from business acquaintances, mostly in England and France, to various people in New York. But neither before nor after had we been particularly close.

Of course, it took only one of these letters to be successful, and it was the last one. Mr. Eckstrom, general counsel of the International Telephone and Telegraph Company (later ITT), told me in no uncertain tones that I needed an American education and, since I had started on law in Vienna, law of the U.S. The schools he recommended were all of the highest rank—and so I came to Virginia. (I only spoke to Mr. Eckstrom once later, very briefly—and never even knew his full name.)

Fortunately the opposite happened in Charlottesville. The first person I encountered there was Hardy Cross Dillard; only fifteen years older than I, he became my role model and close friend. It was he who advised me to look into the possibility of a Ph.D. in political science. I followed his suggestion.

In the army, except for thirteen weeks' basic training and eight weeks spent escorting German residents from Japan back to Europe (see chapter 12), my home was the Twenty-fourth Infantry Division, and with that came friends galore, from Corporal Stephen Targozinski to Generals James A. Lester and Hugh Cort—always singling out Lt. Col. "Jock" Clifford, he of Kiley Ridge fame (see chapter 8), and Max Pitney, with whom I was later reunited, though in reverse order: he was the subordinate, ROTC commandant, and I was the boss (chief of academic affairs of the university), to whom he was accountable.

My first year as a graduate student was highlighted by Robert Kent Gooch's Plato seminar and by the association with George Peek, the only other doctoral candidate to finish that year, with whom I remained friends for as long as he lived.

I considered myself fortunate in 1948 to have landed a job, albeit for only one year, at the University of Kansas. It did not occur to me that I would teach classes there for fifty-five years nor that this would include fifteen years of various administrative assignments, including (twice) duties as interim provost. Among chancellors Franklin D. Murphy (1956–1960), W. Clarke Wescoe (1960–1969), and Gene A. Budig (1981–1994) were notable leaders; fellow administrators I valued included David Ambler, Billy Argersinger, Ed Bassett, Ron Calgaard, Mike Davis and Mike Hoeflich (both in law), Jim Moeser, John Nelson, Ray Nichols, Del Shankel, Emily Taylor, Peter Thompson, and George Waggoner; the list could go on.

Franklin Murphy deserved special mention for it was he, a staunch Republican, who, responding to a request from that Democrat, President Harry S. Truman, recommended me as a possible aide to Mr. Truman in preparation of his memoirs. Out of this came new teaching and research interests for me and friendly associations with such personalities as Dean Acheson and Hubert Humphrey among public figures and Bob Ferrell, Norman Graebner, and Forest Pogue among academics.

Murphy also involved me in his efforts to internationalize the university, with my assignments being both at home and abroad. This resulted in revived contacts in Vienna (Werner Ogris and Walter Rechberger) and Kiel (Hans Hattenhauer).

In the seventies I was asked to serve, as a nonalumnus, on a board set up to bring about a merger of two colleges operated by Benedictines in Atchison, about fifty-five miles from my home. Shortly after the conversion was effected, Abbott Thomas Hartman, who had been elected chairman of the board, was taken ill and resigned. Under the bylaws this placed me in the chairmanship, which I held for seven years (1972–1979); Father Brendan Downey became the new abbot; I had become his friend while he was chaplain to Catholic students at K.U. and my near-neighbor. Father Gerard Senecal was president of the college; some twenty years later his younger brother, Father Barnabas, was elected abbot. I was probably closer to Benedictine monks in my late years than I had been in my growing years in Vienna (see the latter part of chapter 1).

I dedicate this book to those who served with me in the Twenty-fourth Infantry Division, from Hawaii to Japan, from a lowly private to a general's aide: the "Victory Division," "Always the First to Fight."

STEEL HELMET
AND MORTARBOARD

"Home Is the Place Where . . . When You Come to It, They Have to Take You In"

In the summer of 2004 I received a telephone call from the Austrian consulate general in Chicago. Austria, small as it is, cannot afford a plenty of representatives in the United States; the consulate in Chicago covers the Midwest; Kansas is at the far limit of its area of responsibility. To the best of my memory a consul general had visited our state (a small bit of it) in 1984, just as we at the University of Kansas were initiating an exchange of faculty between the law school of Vienna and ours. The young consul general assured me that Vienna had made great progress in the modernization of its "infrastructure," a term that had no meaning to me at the time. I had been asked by the university to share in setting up a European studies program, an effort spearheaded by a young historian, Carl Strikwerda.[1] In the effort to attract both officials and lecturers from the area of our interest, we had approached the various consular representatives in Chicago. The French consul general had been the first to come for what was an entirely successful visit. As a follow-up I contacted the Austrian office and elicited a positive response: part of my itinerary was seeing the Truman Library; calling on the Austrian

1. Now the dean of arts and sciences of the College of William and Mary.

officers attending the U.S. Army Command and General Staff College in Fort Leavenworth; and having coffee with our governor, Kathleen Sebelius. The last seemed the most attractive point.

I had allowed too much time to elapse since we had talked about a possible visit to Kansas by the consul general, Dr. Elizabeth Kehrer; I expected from this telephone call a question about the program. But she surprised me: she wanted to know whether, if she came to Lawrence to present me the Cross of Honor for Science and Art of the Republic of Austria, I would accept that decoration. The thought had never occurred to me; I asked neither why nor how. After a few weeks I began to wonder: had Dr. Kehrer mentioned anything that was expected of me that I had failed to do and, thus, forfeited the medal?

Then a message reached me from my young colleague Richard Levy: the dean (not always friendly to me) had asked him to take charge of the organization of the event which he, the dean, had promised the consul general to do. (The dean had left it to me to choose among several dates, without regard to his calendar.) "Rick," as he is always called, had already done some of the preparatory work. Dr. Kehrer had told him to select a laudator, who, in keeping with European custom, is the person who "lauds" (praises) the honoree. Fred Morrison, whom he had heard me often proclaim as the best of many among students I had taught, had already been contacted. He would be followed by the consul general, who would award the medal. Finally I would be invited to reply.

But reply to what? Neither Professor Morrison (he holds an endowed chair at the University of Minnesota) nor the consul general (who sent me a *vita* that indicated that, in addition to finishing the diplomatic academy, she also had doctorates in law from Cambridge and Paris) could be reached for an advance text. Worse, by 2004 my hearing had deteriorated so badly that I would probably not hear what either said. For help I turned to the *Oxford Dictionary of Quotations* where I found two lines by Robert Frost. From another book I used a line by a nineteenth-century Austrian poet. The rest would come by itself; that, after all, had been the way I had taught for fifty-plus years. Just know the beginning and your end.

The German "Heimat" means more than the English "home." Frost's poetic lines help to approach the German connotation: it's not really home if you perceive it as a place where you are unwelcome to return.

To be sure, for nearly twenty-one years of my life I had resided in one of six different places in Vienna. In that time there had been one place to which I came six days (sometimes) a week for eight successive years: the remarkable middle school run by the Benedictine monks in the city. When I returned to Vienna after twenty-seven years in the United States (and various other places to which the U.S. Army sent me) I went down the long walk from the monastery's entrance to the locked interior doors to the cloister. I encountered an elderly monk; he had been our biology teacher and the school orchestra's conductor; I greeted him by name, Father Amadus; he squinted his eyes, called me by name, and cited St. Benedict's rule that monks should at all times be hospitable. Here was one exception to Robert Frost's poetic definition.

In the same year I experienced another. I had told my wife and my son (then ten years old) about Altaussee. At last I arranged for a rental car and made a reservation at what I remembered as the best hotel, the *Hotel am See*, the hotel at the lake, although I was warned that it was before the season and it was only partially operational. It was late afternoon as I drove up to the hotel's ornate door. A man about my age, dressed in keeping with the local custom, got up from a bench, walked up to me, and hugged me. He was the owner; he and I had gone to the first grade together. He expressed pleasure that we had arrived at sunset when the small lake and its surrounding mountains looked their best. Without difficulty I consider Altaussee another exception to Frost's definition.

Michael Frischmuth, our host (and third-generation owner of the hotel), escorted us to a suite of rooms overlooking the lake. I had described its darkness, but it still surprised my wife. (The color is caused by a unique strain of plankton otherwise found only in a similar phenomenon in the French highlands.) Above the lake, for about five hundred feet, there extends solid evergreen forest; in the evening sun it looked very much like the lake. Above the forest was what looked like a solid chalk wall; the setting sun divided it into a solid red top section and a white lower section. Donna, my Kansas-born wife, marveled at the sight. The following day we wandered around the village (which had about 1,800 inhabitants at the time) nestled among steep mountains. Toward the south, the open country is dominated by the distant view of the *Dachstein*, at almost 10,000 feet, a large permanent glacier on the north side facing the lake, the highest peak in these parts of the Alps and the loveliest setting I know; the *Loser*, the countryside mark with a rock formation on top and mountainous sides all around; the *Salzberg*, the salt mountain that has long been the village's main source of income. Our son was fascinated by the smooth feel of the salt-laden mine walls; Donna and I were treated to tales of how the miners, at the end of World War II, had kept the minions of such Nazi bigwigs as Hermann Goering, who had hidden with his cohorts many of the art treasures amassed during the war from destruction by the Third Reich.

I have no relatives surviving in Altaussee (the name was spelled in two parts [Alt-Aussee] until after World War II), but after I lost my mother to a bicycle accident when I was almost six years, I was sent to spend a year with my grandmother at the lake, and I began healing there. The hotel owner was not the only one to show I had once belonged there and might again.

If my birth mother's death indirectly attached me to Altaussee, it was my stepmother (Denise) who provided the impetus and the resources for what I never suspected she intended to be a virtually lifelong association with Benedictine monks and Benedictine institutions. Tradition has it that the first ducal ruler of the Danube valley, as the river flows through the present territory, Duke Henry II (whom history gives the cognomer *Jasomirgott*, "Yes, so help me Gott," because it was believed that he used that expression after any positive statement he made) persuaded the Irish missionary to the continent, Brother Columba, to start a monastery within boundaries he had chosen for his governmental seat. The monks dedicated their foundation to "Our Lady of the Scots," persons from Ireland being called Scots in those days. A later duke, Rudolph VI, in the fourteenth century caused the future membership (and leadership) to be drawn from local and nearby families. Benedictines being dedicated to education, the monks started internal instruction for future monks and priests. The same Duke Rudolph had started the University of Vienna (1365) and started the practice of having the abbot of the "Scots" serve as rector for the new establishment of higher education. In 1807 Emperor Francis I (of Austria, before 1806 known as Francis II, the last emperor of the German Reich) directed the Scots to start a middle school as a public institution. It became a *Gymnasium*, a school that not only provided instruction in the humanities but also covered a broader area. One of my older confreres, Max Lowenthal, who spent most of his life in the diplomatic service and who eventually served, for many years, as Austrian ambassador in Paris, gave this astute description of the school:

> The selection process seemed to pay little attention to the family's religiosity: By the time I was admitted the majority came from families of basically liberal orientation. There were sons of government officials, industrialists, school teachers, salesmen and farmers. What assembled in the first year was a motley crew indeed. But eight years later they had all become "Scots." That did not mean that they were ideologically or politically of one mind. To be a "Scot" meant to have become imbued with a deep humanism that carried with it both tolerance and openness to continuous learning.[2]

My stepmother wanted me to have this kind of education. But it was not easy. School began at 8:00 A.M. six days a week and normally lasted until 1:00 P.M. with only one break in the midmorning. Usually one afternoon a week was given to drawing or crafts and another to physical education. It was strictly business. There were no extracurricular activities, no student government, no school play. We learned a great deal. I did rather poorly the first three or four years, earning more "satisfactory" (C) than "good" (B) grades and only a rare "very good" (A).

But somehow, things began to fall into place, and in my last four years I was always among the top students in the class. I particularly excelled in history, a subject in which I was acknowledged expert in the class. Dates and sites of battles, genealogies of Europe's great dynasties, the successive phases of the French Revolution—I was the one who knew the answers.

My interest in history was such that when I was fifteen I told my stepmother that I wanted to become a professor of history. At other times, however, I thought of going to the *Konsularakademie*, the entry point for diplomatic service. I am certain that the latter appealed to my parents more than the prospect of having a son in the academic world.

What I learned soon was that in the eight years we spent under the tutelage of the monks we were also affected by the fundamentals of the Rule of Saint Benedict. A few weeks after I finished the comprehensive

2. Maxwell Lowenthal, *Doppeladler und Hakenkreuz: Erlebnisse eines österreichischen Diplomaten* (Innsbruck: Wort und Welt Verlag, 1985), 39, my translation.

examinations leading to *matura*[3] I called, encouraged by the Austrian minister in Warsaw (where my father had lived since 1932), on the Austrian ambassador in London, Baron Georg Franckenstein, the dean of the diplomatic corps in England. His first question was what school I had attended; on my reply "Schottengymnasium" he stood up and shook my hand: "Me too. Call me Georg."[4]

Sixty-nine years later the Austrian consul general sharing my table in Lawrence told me that her entire family was excited: now that the school was turning coeducational, two of her nieces would become first-year "Scots" the following year. I ended my remarks that evening by sending greetings from an "Alt-Schotten" to two future worthy alums of a truly worthy school.

And the consul general smiled. . . .

3. In Germany the comparable examination was (and mostly is) called *Arbitar* (i.e., "going away") while the phrase used in Austria connotes "maturity," presumably to enter a university.

4. After the German takeover of Austria, the ambassador resigned. King George VI of England conferred British citizenship on him and appointed him Sir George Frankenstein.

From Schnitzels to Barbeque

Austria, as many reference books will tell you, covers 83,000 square kilometers (32,000 square miles); Kansas is almost the same size but houses far fewer people: close to three million against more than eight. National news in the U.S. recently focused on a small town two-thirds of the way across Kansas from the east.[1] The storm missed Kinsley, a community of almost like size 25 miles to the north. There, journalists, eager for trivia, would have discovered a highway sign apprising the traveler that he (or she) is 1,250 miles from New York—and also from Los Angeles. Few visitors from abroad ever see that sign. In fact, one of the issues besetting American society is how new immigrants cope or should cope with the immense diversity of the culture they seek to enter.

It is a large country, and from coast to coast its inhabitants do not sound alike. My first exposure to the English language was in the summer of 1935 when I spent six weeks in London and a few weeks traveling about England. In London, on the advice of a young man I had met on the trip, I followed a routine intended to help improve my knowledge of the language. If you purchased an admission ticket to a motion picture theater, you could stay until the day's last show had ended. If I saw the same picture three times, the first time around would help me to learn

1. Greensburg, virtually destroyed by a tornado, May 4, 2007. The home of good friends, I had visited there often.

the plot, the second to acquire some colloquial phrases, and the third to learn some technical ones. Repeating them the next day (or even more often) proved even more useful.

But if you do not use a language it tends to leave you. Three years after that summer in England, I had to repeat the learning—by movies again. That practice did not prepare me for lawyer talk. The rules of law school in America, I soon discovered, was a far cry from the haphazard, casual ways of the University of Vienna. One was expected to attend classes and be prepared to recite when called on. Whether by happenstance or by design, I was the first person to be summoned to this task (or test). The class was "Torts," taught by Leslie Buckler, a lanky, tweed-coated Englishman. As he called my name and asked me what the first case in our book was all about, I could do no more than stare at the words in the book in front of me. "The plaintiff," I read at long last, "was indicted. . . ." A gale of laughter interrupted me: I had pronounced "indicted" to rhyme with "addicted" and "predicted"—but, then, I had never seen the word before and had no knowledge of its meaning.

My embarrassment was painful in the extreme. I am sure I did not hear another word Professor Buckler said that day. I asked myself if, perhaps, going to law school had been a mistake, if I should have looked for some occupation where there was not so much dependence on a complete command of the language.

I had thought that I had made good progress in my use of English during my stay in New York, but here I found it extremely difficult to keep up with conversations, to say nothing of the added obstacle of the regional accent. The boardinghouse table was particularly exasperating. I felt like a complete outsider as the college student jargon floated around me in the muted inflections of southern voices. The subjects of discussions were often incomprehensible to me; the allusions to events and personalities made no sense.

Nor was the food what I was accustomed to. During my stay in New York I had taken my meals either at one of the Horn and Hardart automats or at the YMCA cafeteria. Thus, I was able to choose from among selections I could see, and I had generally taken dishes that at least looked familiar. I had not encountered such southern delicacies as okra or black-eyed peas, had never tasted corn bread or hush puppies or been treated to apple butter as a substitute for the dairy product. Meat was served at Mrs. Carother's boardinghouse in minuscule quantities, and most of it was of poor, stringy quality. Mashed potatoes, on the other hand, were standard fare, and the supply seemed limitless. Kale, turnip greens, and parsnips were part of the menu more often than carrots and string beans. But, then, the average cost of a meal was thirty-seven cents!

New York may have been different but here, in Virginia, I was in a world that was, indeed, new. My life as a student was unlike any experience I had had before—never before had I had to study every day. Classroom discussions were difficult to follow; there was so much taken for granted that I had never heard before!

Tom Noland, the student who had brought me to the place where I lived as well as the one where I ate, continued to befriend me. He urged me over and over again to "take it easy." Everything would, he kept assuring me, fall into place. Rather than spend all my time with the books, he urged me to get some exercise. What sports had I participated in in Vienna? Soccer? There was a soccer club; why didn't I join?

As in most American colleges and universities in those days, soccer at Virginia was a "minor" sport. A faculty member acted as part-time, unpaid coach, and the players paid for their own equipment and chipped in to cover the cost of out-of-town trips. But unlike at most other schools, at Virginia soccer was played by Americans. There was, in fact, only one non-American on the team I joined the following week, a graduate student in history from Scotland by the name of Esmond Wright, later a Member of Parliament and, more recently, the director of the Institute of United States Studies at the University of London and still a good friend of mine.

The team was only moderate, but even so, I never made the starting eleven. What was more important for me was that I made friends on that team. One was an undergraduate, Merrill Bankard, who persuaded me to become active in the International Relations Club. Another was a second-year law student, Bob Greenough. It was he who asked me one day if I could and might want to tutor students in foreign languages; as a former football player and now a part-time assistant coach, he might be able to get me such a job. When I responded in the affirmative, he took me to the university's athletic director, Capt. Norton Pritchett.[2] For fifty cents an hour, I agreed to tutor members of the football team who needed help with foreign languages. In short order, I found myself working four hours a night (seven to eleven), four nights a week, going from Latin to French to German to Spanish (the last language I had never studied myself), tutoring a succession of football players.

Fortunately, by the time this happened I had overcome the trauma of my introduction to Virginia. I had discovered that studying for my law school courses, while it was something that one needed to do daily, was not nearly as strenuous as I had thought at first. The principles of the common law were easier to learn than the minutiae of the Roman law. I retained the details of the cases after just one reading. The more I read, the more my reading speed improved. My ear became attuned to southern voices, indeed I soon came to assimilate the local inflection in my own speech.

The real breakthrough occurred when Warner Janney, Tom Noland's roommate, took me in hand. As a graduate student in English, Janney needed a subject for a required fieldwork exercise in the phonetics of the English language. He was to analyze the speech characteristics of a person of non-English background. Since we were next-door neighbors and ate at the same boardinghouse, it was logical and convenient for him to pick me for his subject. But in the process I learned far more from him than he possibly could have gotten from me. As he collected data on the way I pronounced English words, he also explained to me why my pronunciation differed from standard American speech. More than that, he took me through a series of exercises designed to help a non-English speaker acquire physical bases of articulation used by speakers of American English. I could not have found a better teacher.

What Janney did for me was perhaps, in the long run, of greater help to me than any other assistance that came to me in those early months in Charlottesville. For help and support came to me from many sources, some anonymously. In the latter category was a heavy winter coat that was left for me by a gentleman who, so my landlady reported, did not wish to give his name. Many years later I found out, almost by accident, that the donor had been none other than Dean Ribble of the law school.

2. He had served in the Marine Corps in the "Great War."

Harvey Poe soon came to be closest to me among my classmates. He was a very different kind of person. For instance, he was of my age. He was rather retiring and—although he was an outstanding runner and hurdler—mainly interested in academics.[3] He came from a modest home (his family was distantly related to Edgar Allan Poe) and earned part of his expenses as a dormitory counselor. I spent Christmas with him and his family in Richmond and felt very much at ease with them.

The best friend I made was Father Louis Rowen, the parish priest. Fairly soon after my arrival in Charlottesville, I had begun to help the ushers at the noon mass on Sundays. My schedule of language tutoring meant that I rarely got to bed before 1:00 or 2:00 in the morning, and my class schedule required that I be up by 7:00 at the latest. Sunday was thus a kind of "catch-up" day, and I usually went to the latest mass, which was mainly frequented by students. Quite plausibly, students acted as servers and ushers, and it was Father Louis's practice to invite those who had so assisted at the last mass of the day to join him at the rectory afterward for a light lunch. After some time he asked me to stay later, ostensibly to help him count the collection and post the books. But much of our time was spent in his study upstairs, his great Irish setter stretched out on the floor between our chairs, and there we talked. At times our talk would take on a form of confession that would not be introduced until after the Second Vatican Council: the priest and the parishioner face to face. At times he would encourage me to speak about my past, sensing, perhaps, that talking about it would help me to put it in perspective. At other times we simply talked about the day's news or the previous day's football game. (I had little to contribute to the latter subject: Through my law school colleague Bob Greenough I had gotten a job selling tickets to athletic events, and until I returned from the army in 1947, I never saw the first three quarters of a football game or anything but light-heavies and heavies in boxing).

Father Louis did more than anybody else to give me confidence in my ability to cope with my new surroundings. For one, he never doubted it. Where others would plague me with questions like "How do you like America?'" he took it for granted that, once having come to the United

3. In later years, after he had spent two years as a Rhodes Scholar at Oxford, he was for several years a tutor at St. John's College in Annapolis.

States, I intended to be an American. In retrospect, I am not sure when I made that decision myself, but it must have been during that first year or early in the second. By that time selective service had been enacted. It included one provision of particular applicability to me: as a noncitizen I could claim exception but, if I did, it would ban me from attaining citizenship in the United States. But military service was nothing new to me. I took it for granted that my turn would come.

Finis Austriae

One of the things I learned almost at once is my new abode in the United States was that most people had very little knowledge about the world outside their own country. My new landlord, Mr. Rea, did not know the difference between Austria and Australia. Father Louis arranged for me to talk to some civic groups to explain that this man Hitler, having just swallowed up one country (mine), now wanted another—and could I please draw a map of that one.

My mentor and protector in the law school, Dean Dillard, was an exception. Even though the class in which I saw him daily was "Contracts" (which, clearly for my benefit, he explained was no different than *obligatiunes*, where I would have learned about them if I had not emigrated), he gave the students a good explanation of what the newspapers, reporting from Munich, covered only passingly. When a student thanked him, Dillard smilingly observed that he owed his interest in and knowledge of international relations to his education at the United States Military Academy. When I later asked him what kind of education that was, he, in answering, asked me what Austria did about preparing young men for military careers. It wound up that I was invited to Sunday dinner at the Dillard home where there was another law student (Harvey Poe) who was persuaded to become my volunteer instructor in things American. But first Dillard wanted to learn about officer training in Austria. Obviously I could use myself as an example.

There were no soldiers in either my father's or my mother's family. My father, who was approaching thirty-three when the Great War (as World War I was called) began, had much earlier suffered a serious fracture of the leg. An invalid, he was assigned to work equivalent to what World War II Washington would call the War Production Board. His older brother, Ernest, had taken a job in England and by 1914 was an English subject, married to an English woman. Dad had a much younger brother, Otto, who had been sent to Berlin to school, presumably because it was safer than Vienna during the war. Both of my dad's sisters were married: one to a doctor who spent the war years in a nearby area hospital; the other like my father, disqualified for physical reasons. My mother had only one male sibling, and he was much too young to serve. Her older sister had married a German journalist who abandoned her eventually; I did not meet her until she was an old and very deaf lady. Her younger sister tried to help our family after my mother's death, but my father discouraged that at once, and three years later he remarried. In other families talk might be about life in the military but not in ours. Nor did my parents have friends who were old soldiers, and by the terms of the Treaty of St. Germain (as imposed on the much smaller Austria by the victorious Allies), the new republic was forbidden to have more than 30,000 men in its army, nor could it have planes or tanks. The schools discouraged children from playing soldiers.

Notwithstanding the treaty, Austria denounced the restrictions on its military in 1934. Pre–1919 practices and uniforms were reintroduced. This meant that a graduate of a middle school (students attended until they were nineteen) could volunteer for one year's active duty, during which time he would be assigned to a special officer's training unit. At the end of the year he would be commissioned as a sublieutenant (*Fähnrich*). He would report for six weeks' active duty the following summer, and upon completion of that period be promoted to second lieutenant, with an obligation to perform active duty for three weeks every year until the age of thirty-eight.

Thanks largely to my stepmother's insistence (and her money), I had attended an outstanding secondary school. Completing its course of study entitled one to be admitted to a university, and I had begun the study of law at the University of Vienna. After the first third of the nine-semester curriculum one was eligible to take a set of tests, both written and oral, called the first state examination. It was the first major hurdle on the road to a law degree. Now that military service was mandatory by the age twenty-one, it seemed wise to interrupt my studies right after the first state examination. I volunteered for induction in late September 1937.

My orders directed me to report in September 1937 to the William Barracks (*Wilhelmskaserne*) in Vienna's second district for duty with the Light Field Artillery Regiment No. 1. Our group of recruits, all volunteers for officer training, was assigned to the second battalion, which was the regiment's training unit. We formed the fourth battery while a group of regular conscripts, housed in the same barracks building, were in the fifth. Except for occasional military ceremonies, there was virtually no contact between the two groups.

That our group was the more important of the two was immediately evident from the fact that our battery (normally a captain's billet) was commanded by a major. In fact, Maj. Franz Heckenast was an officer of some renown. In 1934 he had been the president of the court-martial that had tried the Nazis who had killed Chancellor Engelbert Dollfuss and had sentenced them to the gallows. A tall, dignified man in his forties, Major Heckenast was the kind of person who commanded respect when he lowered his voice.

The second-in-command was First Lieutenant Brunner, a short, wiry man who had primary supervision of tactical and physical training while the third officer, First Lieutenant Vogel, handled communications and gunnery training.[1] Brunner and Vogel, both in their late twenties, were well liked and easily approachable while Heckenast was always a rather distant and aloof presence.

The barracks consisted of a series of rooms, each designed to accommodate fifteen men. There was an iron stove in each room and a rough wooden table with two benches. The bedsteads were wooden frames, with planks of wood on which rested straw ticks. Once a week additional straw was distributed, and everybody worked hard to bring his mattress to the tightly compact, squared-off appearance required for Saturday's inspection.

The wash facilities (cold water only) were located in the hall (which was without heat), one for every two rooms. In the basement were three shower units for the nearly two hundred people in the barracks, and they had hot water for only one hour each evening.

1. Gunnery: the management of large guns.

All recruits were issued the same clothing: a summer uniform of rough twill, a winter uniform of heavy wool and an overcoat of the same material, a pair of hobnailed shoes and stiff leather leggings, strips of canvass for the feet (no socks), two shirts of coarse linen and two pair of long underwear of the same material. Notably absent was any kind of rain gear.

The day began, at the ungodly early hour that all armies seem to find necessary for "first call," with a frantic rush to the wash facilities. At the same time, one man from each room went to the mess hall, carrying the canteens of all the men in the room threaded on a stick, to get the breakfast coffee. This concoction, heavy on chicory and light on coffee, was made palatable by a heavy admixture of milk and sugar, and it was hot. Bread was issued twice a week: one black loaf to each man. That was breakfast: bread and coffee (after a fashion).

For the other two meals everybody went to the mess hall. The food was plentiful but of very poor quality: lots of potatoes, watery soups, small portions of stringy and fatty meat. After the first six weeks a number of us arranged to buy our noon meals at the canteen, where the canteen operator's wife was prepared, for a rather modest price, to fix a somewhat tastier (but by no means fancy) fare. This arrangement had the added advantage that we did not have to stand in line for our food and thus gained a few extra minutes of rest before training resumed.

Those who availed themselves of this arrangement were, of course, the people who could afford it. This included most of the occupants of our room. In assigning men to rooms, graduates of the same school had been placed together; our room housed mainly graduates of my school, the *Schottengymnasium*, and of another exclusive school in Vienna, the *Theresianum*, a school originally established by the empress Maria Theresa (1740–1780) almost two hundred years earlier for the education of her court's pages but now a public boarding school with highly selective admission.[2] The result was that we had more titles in our room—two princes, two counts, and four barons—and more money than any other of the rooms in the barracks. One by-product was that the group was

2. Both schools operate to this day in their original premises. My brother Tom, three years my junior and later a professional officer in the United States Army, graduated from the *Theresianum*.

fairly congenial; many of us had known each other before. A decided drawback was that we were deplorably deficient in all housekeeping activities. None of us had ever scrubbed a floor or washed a window, and few had ever polished our own shoes.

Not that the Austrian army intended that its future officers should normally perform such menial tasks. Once the first six weeks of training were behind us, orderlies from other units appeared to take care of washrooms, stoves, floors, and windows. We were allowed to buy tailor-made uniforms for off-duty wear; a few weeks later, we were free to come and go as we pleased as long as we were present for duty hours. I still had the room I had lived in while I was enrolled in law school. Tassilo Hohenlohe (his full name was Tassilo Alexander Franz Josef Karl Prinz von und zu Hohenlohe-Schillingsfürst)[3] had the use of his noble family's twelve-room apartment just across the street. Six mornings a week we shared the cost of a taxi to transport us in style to the day's first formation.

Beside Hohenlohe, the other prince in our room was Karl von Schwarzenberg. His great-grandfather had the rare distinction of having defeated Napoleon in battle (at Aspern in 1809), entitling him to a heroic equestrian statue on a square bearing his name, just off the Ringstrasse in the center of Vienna. Karl was about five or six years older than the rest of us. He had been active in the political organization supporting the government (as I had been), and we had met before in that context.

Politics was, however, totally absent in the relationships of our group. Basically, those who had been placed together in this room found it easy to socialize together. On Sunday mornings, between eleven and twelve, we could be found parading up and down the fashionable *Kärtnerstrasse* (now a pedestrian mall) in the center of the city in our tight-fitting gray tunics, riding breeches, and high-polished boots. Although we were not authorized to do so, everyone carried a saber; and, whether assigned to the mounted (as opposed to the motorized) section or not, everybody sported spurs.

For formal social occasions the accepted uniform (which everyone in our room had acquired by Christmas) consisted of a dark brown tunic

3. His great uncle owned a hunting lodge in Altaussee, and Tassilo and I had known each other from grade school days.

with red stand-up collar and red sleeve cuffs and black trousers with red piping at the seams. Everything was snugly tailored, forcing a rigid military stance even if one stood relaxed.

As the weeks continued, training shifted gradually from physical activities to classroom work, with gunnery taking up much of the time. Interspersed was guard duty (I spent Christmas Eve that year walking around one of the transmission towers of the government-owned radio system on a hill just north of the city) and field exercises. In January we spent two weeks on a snow-covered artillery range in the mountains putting our newly acquired classroom knowledge into practice.

Events began to overtake us as we returned from this training period. There was a rare letter from my father who had been living in Warsaw (Poland) since 1933 where he represented mostly British banking interests in efforts to assist Polish debtors to meet their obligations. He wrote that the diplomats with whom he socialized were increasingly pessimistic about the future of Austria. I replied that I had not noticed anything of the sort in Vienna, that in fact Chancellor Kurt von Schuschnigg's most recent speech had offered a decidedly hopeful picture and had received a positive response.

Dad's informants knew, of course, both more and better than I. In early February, Schuschnigg had, under severe pressure, visited Hitler at the latter's country place above Berchtesgaden. The Austrian press had not reported much detail, but newspapers abroad had carried stories that at this meeting Schuschnigg had been subjected to incredible threats and pressures. In the end he had agreed to remove virtually all restraints on the activities of the Austrian Nazis. The press had linked this event to the shake-up of the high command of the German army which Hitler had engineered just a few days earlier: Some foreign analysts concluded that Hitler had decided to put an end to Austria as an independent nation and had removed generals who opposed such a drastic course of action.

None of this, however, was known to us. But late in February some of our comrades-in-arms began to reveal themselves as members of the Nazi Soldiers' Circle, an organization which, until then, had been outlawed but was now allowed to operate openly. Heinz Rabner, who had the bunk next to mine, turned out to be the leader of the cell in our battery.[4] Suddenly, the pleasant atmosphere in our group disintegrated. Now it seemed to be more important whether you were "brown" or "red-white-and-red."

The crisis came in the second week in March. On Wednesday, March 9, Chancellor Schuschnigg announced that the following Sunday there would be a plebiscite on the single question of whether Austrian citizens favored the continued existence of an independent Austria. The question had all of the characteristics of a "God, country, and motherhood" issue; the time element would preclude any effective internal agitation against the affirmative. Once the people had spoken, Schuschnigg assumed that he would be able to face Hitler with confidence that his position had public support. It was an ingenious ploy, and it would prove the last public initiative of a desperate man.

All over Austria the Nazis now took to the streets. The government reacted on Thursday (March 10), calling army reservists to active duty and ordering all army units to remain in their barracks in readiness. The Nazis stepped up their agitation against the plebiscite. In Graz, the capital of Styria and Austria's second-largest city, they seized the city hall and hoisted the swastika flag from its tower.

Early Friday morning our unit was called out and told that we would occupy alert stations. We were issued ammunition and ordered into position. Whoever had made the assignments knew what he was doing. Heinz Rabner and others who had revealed themselves as active Nazis were assigned to kitchen and supply details. Schwarzenberg and I were sent to man an antiaircraft machine gun on the roof of a tall building overlooking the major bridge across the Danube.

We remained there until nearly 8:00 P.M. when a corporal came to take us and our machine gun back to the barracks. The word, he said, was that it was all over: Schuschnigg had resigned and the German army would enter Austria in the morning. I remember that Schwarzenberg said, "God help us all!" I do not know that I said anything; there was just a sense of overwhelming, dry emptiness.

When we got back to the barracks, Lieutenant Brunner was seated at Heckenast's desk, wearing a red armband with the black swastika in a

4. Not his real name. It was unconfirmed to us that he was lost in combat in Russia.

white circle. Rabner, sporting a similar armband, assured Schwarzenberg and me that we would continue to be good friends and that we had nothing to fear. Colonel Heckenast (he had been promoted in January), he told us, had been arrested as had one of the warrant officers. Heckenast, he said, had blood on his hands (the court-martial conviction of the Dollfuss murderers), and the warrant officer had apparently been the man who knew our political leanings so well that he could indicate who was politically reliable and who was a Nazi. But people like Schwarzenberg and I would find that the new government was neither vindictive nor arbitrary. I had no doubt that Rabner was sincere; I may even have wanted to believe him.

But events moved more swiftly and perhaps unfolded differently than even Rabner might have expected. On Sunday, March 13, the day on which Schuschnigg had planned to see the independence of Austria affirmed by its people, Austria ceased to be. Arthur Seiss-Inquart, who, at Hitler's insistence, had replaced Schuschnigg as chancellor, announced a decree that made Austria a part of the German Reich. Within days, Hitler would order that the name Austria was to be used no longer: the area was now the German Reich's *Ostmark.*[5] By Monday (March 14), German soldiers were everywhere (each, interestingly enough, equipped with a phrasebook to help him get along with the Austrian dialect and the rather significantly different vocabulary). The following day, the German government directed the absorption of the Austrian army into the *Reichswehr*; the very next day all members of what had been the Austrian *Bundesheer* were to swear personal loyalty to Adolf Hitler.

I asked Schwarzenberg what he intended to do. We agreed that it would be hypocritical to take the oath. We talked about the consequences. The newspapers, now all Nazi-controlled, made it very clear that "enemies of the German people" were being rounded up in large numbers. The Hotel Metropol in the center of the city had been made into the headquarters of the Secret State Police (the *Gestapo*), and freely circulating rumors had it that from there hundreds (perhaps even thousands) of people were daily dispatched to concentration

5. Even that name was soon proscribed. If any reference had to be made to the former Austria, it had to be called the "*Alpen-und Donaugaue*," the districts of the Alps and the Danube.

camps in Germany. Karl told me that six members of his family had already been taken away. Given our (his and mine) past political activity, swearing an oath to be loyal to Hitler would protect neither of us very long.[6]

There were a few others in our barracks who, either because of previous political activity or because they would fall under the proscriptions of the German racial laws, were in the same position. Some of them agreed to do as we had decided to do: We would not raise our right hands and we would not speak the words of the oath.

Within half an hour after the oath ceremony all of us were standing at rigid attention before Lieutenant Brunner. Was it true, he asked, that we had not taken the oath? When we answered in the affirmative, he asked if we understood the enormity of our refusal; as our friend, he would give us five minutes to reconsider. Two in our small group indeed changed their minds, but the rest (including myself) persisted. We would, said Brunner, be relieved of all duties and be restricted to the barracks until he received instructions on what to do with us.

That evening Rabner talked to me at length, trying to get me to change my mind. I told him that I was certain that, sooner or later, my past political activities would lead to my arrest and that I could not and would not deny my past. He talked about the providential mission of the Germans; I replied that, to my knowledge, every nation on earth could, and usually did, believe that it was uniquely destined and that Hitler's course was bound to result in war. Yes, he said, of course it will, "and our victory will fulfill our destiny: it will make us masters of the earth." I remember what I replied: "Neither you nor I will ever see the day."

A week later our little group of recalcitrants was ordered to turn in its uniforms and equipment. We were given documents that indicated that we had been transferred to the reserve, subject to call-up for service

6. What made my position precarious was that in the preceding summer I had discovered that several of the local leaders of the youth organization in which I had a minor function were members of the (then illegal) Nazi Party. Among those arrested on my report was a nephew of Ernst Kaltenbrunner who had emerged, at the time of the *Anschluss*, as the top SS officer in Austria and had been placed in charge of all internal security. His subsequent rise in the Nazi hierarchy landed him among defendants in the principal war crimes trial of Nuremberg where he was found guilty of crimes against humanity and sentenced to death by hanging.

"without arms" (i.e., with a labor unit). Schwarzenberg and I took a taxi into the inner city and had dinner together. I never saw him again.

A letter from my father alerted me that a Mrs. Polturak would get in touch with me, and within a day she did invite me to come at my earliest convenience to her nearby apartment. She was Viennese, but Mr. Polturak was a Pole who, on Polish government business, traveled to Vienna weekly, on a diplomatic passport. He had agreed to carry messages between my father and me, but all contact would be through the wife.[7] Through this channel I received railroad tickets to Warsaw for me and my brothers, but I was also instructed to sell as many of my possessions (clothes, books, my stamp collection) as possible and pay the remaining bills for my brothers' tuition and board. I had already submitted to the local police requests for all three of us, separately and together, to travel abroad. On two occasions I was picked up. The first time I was stopped by a university student whom I had come to know at the student government (where I thought him a member of the Catholic organization but he now wore a brown uniform). I was released. The second one an inquiry by the criminal police, but I was able to refute a charge of theft from the law students' organization.

At last we were given the exit permits, and I was able, through the Polturak channel, to alert my parents in Warsaw to our plans for departure from Vienna. That night, as I have related in my preface, occurred the episode of Gustl Zahourek's visit. Acting on Gustl's alert (and a promise that his girlfriend would see to it that my brother Steve boarded the express train for Warsaw), I elected to take a local train to a place near the March River and then cross the water under cover of darkness. Steve and I reunited where the express train had its first stop in Czechoslovakia. We were with our parents in Warsaw that afternoon.

One of the first things I learned there was that, thanks to the American consul general who had befriended me during my previous visits with my parents, a visa to enter the United States awaited me. My father had arranged for my brother Tom to enter the university in

7. After Germany's invasion, Polturak joined the Polish army and was able to escape through the Balkans to southern Italy where persons in his position came to form a Polish division that fought on the side of the Allies. He died in combat. I saw his wife again in 1975 in a village near Salzburg where she ran a boutique—and told me her family's history.

Grenoble in France while Steve, the youngest, would enter a boarding school in England. My father saw this dispersal of the family as temporary, to last just until this Hitler phenomenon would have run its course. Little did he know.

Dad had bought passage for me on a Polish ship. I arrived in New York on August 20, 1938; a month later I was in Charlottesville, a first-year law student at the University of Virginia. By the end of my second year there I had reached two important decisions: one was that I should remain in the United States, regardless of what happened in Europe; the other was that, after law school, I should work toward a Ph.D. in political science, focusing on American constitutional law. Thus, when I registered for the draft I did not claim the exemption available to noncitizens; had I done so, I would have been permanently barred from attaining American citizenship. But, as an alien, I had no option but to await the call of the Selective Service board.

My brother followed me to the United States a year later. I saw him in the spring of 1940 when our parents arrived in New York; they had fortunately been on vacation in France. I next saw Tom in the Philippines. We were both in the army, and he visited me in a hospital. He was suffering from a case of jaundice. Our youngest brother we did not learn of for the longest time. He served in the British army and remained in the United Kingdom, with a British brigade, until 1957. The family remained essentially dispersed.

Fort Bragg, North Carolina

In September 1942 I received the draft board's notice of induction and learned I was to take a physical examination in three weeks. When I reported, I was found to be physically fit for military service, and by midafternoon of the same day, I, along with a dozen or so draftees from Charlottesville, was on a bus headed for Petersburg, Virginia, and Camp (now Fort) Lee, the army's reception center for the state. There we went through the expected routine: We were given army clothing, army haircuts, army immunizations, army tests. Then came the waiting. We were introduced to the rudiments of close-order drill and that essential activity of military forces the world over called "policing the area." Any day, we were told repeatedly by the sergeant in charge of our barracks, we would be "shipped out" to the next destination, a replacement training center.

It was on the third or fourth day, as we were lined up to begin the inevitable search of the grassy areas for cigarette butts and scraps of paper, that the sergeant told me to report to a certain building in the administrative area. When I arrived there, a grizzled master sergeant told me to take a seat and wait. Close to half an hour had elapsed when he called me to his desk and told me that I would be going into the adjoining room to report to "the lieutenant," and he instructed me in the proper way to do this.

But when I walked into the next room, I almost forgot what I had to do: I knew the man behind the desk; he was a graduate student from Johns Hopkins University with whom I had shared a couple of beers at the political science convention earlier in the year. When I expressed my pleasure at finding him here and thanked him for having sent for me, he quickly set me straight: *He* had not sent for me; I had been sent to him because it was his job to interview all those new inductees whose scores on the Army General Classification Test were above 168. Many of the people with such high scores (the top 2 percent) either had poor coordination or were otherwise suitable only for highly specialized tasks. My score, he told me, was 178 (out a maximum of 180). That was the highest he had seen in the four months that he had performed this duty; it qualified me, he said, for assignment to virtually any branch of the service. He could, for instance, arrange to have me sent to the military intelligence training center at Camp Holabird in Maryland where, with my knowledge of German and French, I would readily qualify for training as a translator or interpreter for military intelligence. I deferred. I said I would rather be sent to a combat arm, and I mentioned my brief experience as an artillery trainee in the Austrian army. He leafed through some papers on his desk: "There is a shipment of trainees going to Fort Bragg in three days. That's an artillery training center. I'll see to it that you are on the list."

To be sure, three days later I found myself among several hundred others on a troop train destined for (though, of course, we had not been told so) Fort Bragg, North Carolina. Darkness had fallen when we arrived, and we were herded into a cavernous hall where, along with men who had arrived from other reception centers, we were given a written test, mostly on trigonometry and algebra. Then we were marched to a barracks area and, at last, allowed to bed down.

The next morning was spent in the usual desultory activities: close-order drill, physical exercise, and, of course, "policing the area." After lunch we were called out with all of our belongings and redistributed to different training units. My new unit was made up of those who, we were promptly told by a young lieutenant, had scored highest on the test the night before. Potentially, every one of us was officer material, and we had been grouped together in order to give us some special training that would help qualify us for Officer Candidate School (OCS). It probably also made it easier to evaluate us, but that he did not tell us.

The battery area consisted of an administrative building and four barracks, each of two floors. The men in my barracks came mostly from New York and New Jersey. They were a bright and lively group although, interestingly enough, I was the only one who had graduated from college or had a comparable education. (I assumed, I think correctly, that this was a reflection of the prevailing impression that battleships were safer in modern wartime than foxholes, and the fact that the navy made it much easier than the army for a college graduate to receive a commission.)

The oldest man in our group was a tailor from Brooklyn, Joe Mazarowitz. Thirty-two years old, he was also the shortest man in the unit and had to put forth superhuman effort in physical training. He was an Orthodox Jew who never failed, at the proper times, to put on his prayer shawl and his phylacteries and say his prayers. It was the first time in my life that I had seen anyone do this. Mazarowitz was witty and an incredibly hard and willing worker. If there was work to be done, he was always the first to pitch in. I think everyone in our group liked him. Eventually, he was killed in action in North Africa, as was Chick Parslow, a happy-go-lucky fellow from Montclair, New Jersey, who was our self-appointed cheerleader. I enjoyed the company of Tibor Mikes, a Hungarian who had been drafted out of his sophomore year at Princeton. Another whom I liked was Herb Merrill, a postal clerk from Washington, D. C. But my best friend quickly became Sam Gilner, a brash but jovial fellow who had driven a truck for his father's laundry in Bergen, New Jersey, before he was drafted and who quickly emerged as the leader of our little group.

We were a congenial aggregation, but even here I was different. I had a law degree. I had taught at a university. On the other hand, I had not played football or baseball or golf, or done anything else to keep physically fit. But, like my compatriots, I had done a good deal of walking. Perhaps for that reason I found out that I was as tough as any of them, but in many ways I lacked the agility most of them had acquired in the typical American high school setting. (Even Mikes, the Hungarian, had been through the major part of his schooling in the United States.) When we went on a twenty-five-mile forced march I was likely to be last after the first five miles but among the first five or ten when we reached the end. On the obstacle course, the jumps were nearly my undoing, but the distance to be covered never bothered me.

I had no trouble at all with the artillery training as such. Because all of us were expected to go to Officer Candidate School, we were given a considerable amount of schooling in gunnery—essentially applied trigonometry, at which I was good. The techniques were, basically, no different from the ones I had learned in the Austrian army, and I mastered the subject quickly.

"Gunnery" is a general concept, encompassing everything from theories of ballistics to design and behavior of fuses and modes of transportation of heavy weapons. Typically countries would develop aspects of gunnery that would compensate for failures in their most recently fought wars.

This tendency was particularly evident when a nation's political stance was opposed to preparation for war. To be sure, once the United States entered World War I, patriotic sentiment ran high, but it was only after the fighting ended that it became commonly known that American artillery had proven ineffective and American gunners had been forced to turn to French equipment—the "French 75" (which the French had developed after their defeat by Prussia in 1870).

American military professionals sought funds to modernize their equipment but encountered public (and congressional) opposition. (The most spectacular instance was the court-martial in 1925 of Gen. William "Billy" Mitchell for his persistent public advocacy of military aviation.) Less public retribution for efforts at reform of the military was common. The result was that the American army entered World War II inadequately armed and prepared. Its first major encounter on the ground with the enemy (in North Africa in the fall of 1942) was a series of disasters usually attributed to poor equipment and insufficient training.

By this time I had finished basic training.

The men in our battery had been instructed to apply for Officer Candidate School. We took tests, underwent physical examinations, and some of us were called for interviews before a board of officers. As our basic training approached its end, a few of those who had already been interviewed received orders to the field artillery school at Fort Sill, Oklahoma. Only one in our little group was among those so selected (and, rightly or wrongly, we suspected that the fact that his father was a Regular Army colonel might have had something to do with this).

The day our basic training ended we were told that we would be shipped out. The young lieutenant who had been our commanding officer assured us that we were still considered officer material, that our applications to OCS were still active, and that we could expect to be sent to Fort Sill from our next duty station.

That turned out to be Fort Meade, Maryland, but we quickly discovered that it was merely a holding area from which we would be sent on. Yes, our OCS papers were still in order and would certainly be considered once we got to our next destination. About a week later, half of us were shipped out, including Mazarowitz, Mikes, and Parslow. They went to North Africa (as I found out from Mikes after the war) as replacements for the Ninth Infantry Division.

A few days later the rest of us was told to pack barracks bags and climb aboard another troop train. This one went clear across the country in six long days of less-than-comfortable travel. Once a day (usually during the hours of darkness) the train would pull on to a siding, we would all be told to get out, and there would be a half hour of callisthenics. There were, of course, no shower facilities aboard, and all of us were fairly smelly by the time the train finally reached the San Francisco area. We were marched from the train to a ferry and shortly found ourselves on Angel Island,[1] in the middle of the bay and next to Alcatraz Island (sometimes called Devil's Island), the site of the notorious prison. Angel Island had been built up as the Pacific coast equivalent of Ellis Island, a location to screen out aliens. Renamed Fort McDowell, it was now just another army processing point.

A few of the men were pulled out and sent off in varying directions. I was interviewed by an intelligence officer who seemed to be mostly interested in knowing why, with my knowledge of foreign languages, I was not at Camp Holabird (and did not want to be). I am not sure that I could articulate my reason.

We had arrived in heavy winter uniforms and now received additional cold-weather gear. The implication was obvious: We were headed for duty in Alaska. In June 1942, the Japanese had seized Attu and Kiska, two

1. A brief illustrated story on Angel Island, its history and its present status, appeared in *Smithsonian* vol. 37, no. 2 (May 2006).

small islands in the Aleutians and part of the Territory of Alaska. The islands were not recaptured until May and August 1943, respectively.

Few Americans would have been able to locate what the media promptly described as added threats to the nation's security. The *Chicago Tribune* asked editorially when the War Department would send a ranking general to mount a counteroffensive and eject the Japanese from Alaska. On the day when our group, dressed for combat in the arctic, was herded onto a troopship, the army chief of staff, Gen. George C. Marshall, let it be known that he might increase the troop unit based at Anchorage, Alaska, but he refused to reveal the rank of any new commander. A jokester in our midst opined that, there being five hundred of us recruits, one acting first sergeant would probably suffice.

Once we had cleared the Golden Gate, the small group that escorted us, always evading all questions about our destination, began to prepare us for the fact that most of us would be commingling with "old soldiers," men who had seen years of service and—and this point was reiterated—had already learned the new equipment and its use. This began to make more sense when, on the third morning, we realized that, under cover of darkness, our ship had changed course and was now heading southwest. We were headed not to Alaska, but Hawaii.

Oahu, Territory of Hawaii

Five days later Diamond Point hove into view, and a few hours later, still dressed in our winter uniforms, we stood, perspiring profusely, on a railroad siding on a Pearl Harbor pier. We clambered into boxcars, and the narrow-gauge train began climbing toward the interior of the island. Our destination, we had been told, was Schofield Barracks.

I had never seen an old, established U.S. Army post (neither at Fort Bragg nor at Fort Meade had I ever gotten to the main post area). For the first few days we had little to do. We spent the days at various labor details: stacking cases of beer in a post exchange warehouse, digging graves at the cemetery, painting a recreation building. A weekend intervened and Gilner, Merrill and I wandered around the post. I discovered the post library, but I was not allowed to check out books as I had not yet been assigned to a unit. Still, I was pleased to know that there was such a thing and that it was well stocked. (As it turned out, I never got to use it.)

Then Merrill was called out and assigned to the army postal unit at Fort Shaffter, the army's headquarters for administration. Given his civilian experience, it made sense, but it meant that now only Sam Gilner and I were left out of our old Fort Bragg gang. Two days later we, too, were separated.

The entire group of replacements was ordered to assemble in the large square in front of our barracks prepared to move out. A tall lieutenant stood in the middle of the square: We were, he announced, all assigned to the artillery of the Twenty-fourth Infantry Division. There were four battalions, and we would now learn to which of these each of us was to go.

A sergeant began to call out names "all of you, over there, to the 11th Field Artillery 13th Field Artillery [there went Sam Gilner] 52nd 63rd right face, forward march!" My name had not been called. Three other men were also waiting, but when the sergeant checked his roster, it turned out that they had failed to hear when their names were called. The tall lieutenant came over to me: "You must be Heller. Get in my car: You are going to Divarty headquarters." I did not know what "Divarty" meant, but then, throughout our basic training, we had been told over and over again that "yours is not to reason why. . . ."

"Divarty," it turned out, was short for "Division Artillery," and I was headed to Headquarters Battery, Twenty-fourth Division Artillery. It would be my address for the next *four* years.

Since World War I, the United States Army had maintained one major combat unit in Hawaii, rather unimaginatively called the Hawaiian Division. In 1941, the army changed from the "square" infantry division of four regiments (plus supporting elements) to "triangular" divisions. There were now three regiments of infantry, each with three battalions of three companies, and so on, all the way down to three squads per platoon. Since Hawaii's two National Guard infantry regiments (the 298th and the 299th) had been called into federal service, there were now six infantry regiments in the territory, and they were divided among two divisions (the Twenty-fourth and the Twenty-fifth), which replaced the old Hawaiian Division. In this realignment (which had taken effect in the fall of 1941), the headquarters units had been filled up first and the line units brought up to strength as the draft and enlistments provided personnel. Our shipment (nearly five hundred men) had been designed to fill up the artillery units of the Twenty-fourth Division. (The Twenty-fifth had been brought to full strength first and had already left for the southwest Pacific where it would soon be heavily involved in the fighting on Guadalcanal in the Solomon Islands.)

Headquarters battery, division artillery was at full strength. Of course, I did not know that at the time. How I came to be the first draftee in the battery was not told me until three years later, by the same general who commanded the Twenty-fourth Division Artillery at the time I joined it, Brig. Gen. James A. Lester. "Jimmy," as everyone called him behind his back, was a gentle person and a first-class professional. (His previous assignment had been as assistant commandant of the Field Artillery School at Fort Sill, Oklahoma, in effect, the school's academic dean). As I quickly learned, he was greatly respected by the officers and well liked by the enlisted men. When, in mid-1944, he was transferred to Fourteenth Corps everyone was sorry to see him go. He returned to us, however, late in 1945, now a two-star general, to be our division commander.

By that time, of course, the fighting was over, and we were in Japan. I was now a second lieutenant and had been ordered to report to the division commander. "Jimmy" asked me to serve as one of his two aides. But army regulations at the time (and, for all I know, still today) provided that, if an officer had served one tour of duty as a general's aide, he could decline to accept another such appointment, and it could not be held against him. I had just finished serving as aide to Brig. Gen. Hugh Cort, until recently our artillery commander. I was seriously thinking about staying in the army. I needed other kinds of experience so, despite my devotion to General Lester, I declined. He then asked me if I knew how I happened to find myself in division artillery headquarters in the first place.

He explained that when this large group of replacements arrived, his executive officer, Col. Homer Kiefer (later a two-star general and division commander himself), had decided that he should personally supervise the allocation of the largest-ever batch of recruits to the four battalions that made up the "Divarty." It was he who had noticed my test score. General Lester related that Kiefer had come into his office with my Form 20 (the enlisted man's qualifications record) in his hand and had offered the opinion that here was somebody who might be worth a closer look. "He is either one of these eggheads who can't tie their own shoelaces or he is the guy we want to groom to be our key noncom by the time we hit the thick of the fighting." General Lester had agreed, and that was how I found myself that day in Schofield Barracks being turned over by the tall lieutenant (Al Early, a recent Texas A&M graduate) to the first sergeant of Headquarters Battery, an old-timer by the name of Bullard who had fought in the Forty-second "Rainbow" Division under Gen. Douglas MacArthur during the First World War.

The spacious barracks area of Headquarters Battery was almost empty. The entire division was in field positions on the northern half of the island, and only clerical and supply personnel were still in Schofield Barracks where I would spend a few days for processing.

Almost all of the men who were in the barracks had also been there on the day the Japanese attacked the island.[1] They welcomed the opportunity to impress a rookie with their tales. They were all Regular Army men. Next to the first sergeant, the oldest and the one with the longest service was Private First Class Alex.[2] He had, I was told, repeatedly declined promotion, simply because he had managed to carve out an almost ideal existence for himself: His duty assignment was, believe it or not, permanent latrine orderly! He hired two small boys to do the work. He would check their arrival in the morning and then return in the afternoon to make sure that everything had been done properly.

Every two weeks he would find himself on guard duty. In a tradition going back to the Revolutionary War, the soldier who presented the best appearance at guard mount would be designated by the commander of the guard to serve as the colonel's (or general's) orderly. Instead of walking post, he would sit outside the general's office, available to run errands or do whatever else was needed. Alex had elevated preparations for guard duty to an art: He wore a tailor-made uniform and a pair of highly polished boots (which he used for nothing else). To avoid getting wrinkles in his uniform or dust on his boots, he not only had two men help him get into his trousers and boots, but he also had them carry him to guard mount. It never failed: Alex was always the orderly selected, and with that came the privilege of a three-day pass. Since every man was entitled to a three-day pass once a month, Alex would spend 20 percent of every month on pass. He had long been living with a woman in Honolulu and had either two or three children with her. For all practical purposes, he commuted to the army.

1. It has become customary to refer to December 7, 1941, because of what happened that day, as "Pearl Harbor Day." In fact the Japanese attack on Oahu was two-pronged: one target was the naval base; the other, the army installations in the center of the island, Schofield Barracks and the neighboring Hickam Airfield, hence the Twenty-fourth Division's claim to be "the first to fight." But historians are unlikely to change what happened to "the battle of Oahu."

2. His actual last name. I never knew his full name.

Of course, things had changed even for Alex when the war started. For one, with most of the men in the field, he had lost a major source of extra income that came from running the games in the day room. For another, he had to travel back and forth in uniform, with rifle, steel helmet, and gas mask. But he had virtually no professional qualifications, and the captain and the first sergeant were quite willing to have him continue in his ways. (He remained with us until a few days after our first combat action when he was sent back to Hawaii—and retired.)

On the third or fourth day the first sergeant took me to Poamaho Gulch, where the division command post was located in a concrete underground installation. The personnel were housed in heavily camouflaged wooden shacks, with mosquito screens for windows, along both sides of the gulch. I had been assigned to the headquarters section, but because that section's hut was full, I was told to move in with some men from the communications platoon. I quickly discovered that I had to learn a new vocabulary: That evening, as some of the men were engaging in a game of blackjack, I learned more profanity than I had ever heard before, and I have not had to add much since.

The headquarters section consisted of the men who worked directly for the general and the staff officers. A master sergeant, Carmel Wallace, was the noncommissioned officer in charge of the section, and he had the job title of operations sergeant. A staff sergeant served as principal clerk for the officer handling personnel (S-1) and supply (S-4) matters (then Lt. Early). Two sergeants worked under Wallace, each on duty for eight hours. There was a stenographer for the general, a draftsman, and three other clerks (of whom I was now one).

The officers were an impressive group. General Lester, a small man of rather delicate features and with the soft voice of the southerner, was almost a father figure. Colonel Kiefer I did not get to know because he was soon transferred back to the States to take command of the artillery of a newly formed division. He was succeeded as executive officer by Lt. Col. Cornelis de W. W. "Tommy" Lang, a likeable, energetic officer. The operations officer (S-3) was Lt. Col. Livingston Taylor, and a finer officer I have simply never known. Lang and Taylor had been classmates (and friends) at West Point. The last of the key people was the assistant S-3 (later the S-2 [intelligence]), Capt. Paul Keating, who had, until the year before, held the job now filled by Master Sergeant Wallace. He had been an enlisted man in the Regular Army for a number of years but had earned a reserve commission and eventual promotions in the reserve while he was working as a sergeant. He knew the job inside out, and I found him a superb teacher, if a rather dour individual.

There were three officers who were assigned to the battery (rather than the headquarters). One of these was the survey officer while the other two were primarily concerned with the battery and with the communications duties. Shortly afterward a fourth officer was assigned to the battery, and later on headquarters acquired a separate position of a communications officer as well as two officers whose principal duty it was to fly the two L-4 (Piper Cub) liaison planes that had been assigned to the headquarters for aerial reconnaissance and fire control.

The battery was divided into three platoons. The battery headquarters platoon, headed by the first sergeant, consisted of personnel of the orderly and supply rooms and a machine gun section (for local security). The communications platoon, with a section each for wire communications, radio communications, and the message center, was headed by a master sergeant as communications chief. The operations platoon, led by the operations sergeant, also had three sections: headquarters, survey, and meteorological. The sergeants were all men who had been in the army for five years or longer. Even some of the privates had been in the service for ten or more years (and several had themselves been noncommissioned officers but had been reduced in grade for a variety of misdeeds). After the war, James Jones wrote a highly successful novel, later made into a no less successful motion picture, both entitled *From Here to Eternity*. Jones had served in, and was describing, our sister unit, the Twenty-fifth Division, but I can attest to the fact that his characters are not atypical "old army" men.

Initially my duties fell into two distinct parts. At 5:30 P.M., or whenever I finished my evening meal, I reported to the underground command post where one of the two sergeants and I were expected to remain awake until midnight and respond to any telephone calls that might come in. There was a shelf on which there was one telephone for each of the four artillery battalions. The phones were connected with observation posts that dotted the mountains and hills clear around the northern half of the island. Since the island was under total blackout and the use of boats or any other form of shipping after dark was prohibited, the observation posts' principal duty was to report any light they might see on the water. We would then plot the location and notify the duty officer (one of the officers always slept on a cot in the executive officer's office) who would, if necessary, alert a nearby unit to investigate. In fact, virtually all reports we received were false alarms.

The sergeants in charge of the night shifts were both Texans. If there was nothing to do, Stewart (I do not recall their first names) would simply doze off. Thomas was a different type. He hoped to make it to OCS and would spend his time in study. We soon did it together. I taught him trigonometry and, in turn, learned a lot from him about "army ways."

On the nights when I was on with Stewart I would study the papers on the officers' desks. I discovered quickly that the army had rather specific ways of organizing its paperwork. Taylor's training directives and practice field orders were models. Keating's problems for field exercises were always worked out to the last detail. I learned a great deal just from reading the papers on their desks. I also discovered that Thomas played a double role: he was also an agent of the Counter-Intelligence Corps (CIC) and as such wrote regular reports on individual members of our unit.

As a member of the armed forces I was eligible for American citizenship after three (instead of the regular five) years in the United States. As soon as I had determined that I was not about to be shipped to still another assignment I filed my application, and when the day came for me to be sworn in, I asked Thomas and Stewart to serve as my witnesses.

We went to the United States District Court in Honolulu for the ceremony. There were about thirty future citizens in the courtroom, all in military uniform of one kind or another. A representative of the Immigration and Naturalization Service called the roll and then presented the group to the judge for the administration of the oath. The judge delivered a brief address, in which he noted that we were already serving the country that now would be ours, and then inquired if anyone wished to have his name legally changed at this time. A sailor raised his hand first; his was a long Polish name, and both his first and middle names were also strictly Polish; I sensed that the judge was somewhat surprised when all the sailor asked was to have his first and middle names transposed. My request was much simpler and clearly the kind the judge expected: I asked to be known henceforth by the Anglicized form of my first name and by the middle name I had assumed (Howard), indicating that I had used both since my arrival in the United States. Then, after I had repeated the oath of allegiance to the United States of America, "foreswearing all allegiance formerly owed to any king, sovereign, or nation," I proudly took my two sergeants out to a lunch of steak and the works; a private's pay at that time was thirty dollars a month.

Of course, even on this festive day, my duty in the command post began right after dinner. Our relief came on duty at midnight. But my rest was brief; I would be called at 5:30, along with the men who were on kitchen police for that day (a chore which, of course, also came to me, on the average of once every ten days). I would eat an early breakfast and then carry a pail of hot water to the hut occupied by General Lester. The general used a small part of the water to shave; with the remainder and a stiff brush I scrubbed the floor of the hut while the general went through his ablutions and got dressed. What I did not realize at the time was the significance of the general's regularly engaging me in conversation. I interpreted that as just one other manifestation of what the other men had told me: that "Jimmy" Lester was really a nice guy. In fact, of course, he was trying to find out what he should do with me.

Once I had finished my task in the general's hut, made my bunk, and attended to other chores, I was expected to report to Corp. Stephen Targozinski. "Targo," as everyone called him, was a blond giant of about six feet, six inches. He had been the heavyweight wrestling champion of the army; in fact, he was so strong that he could lift a .50 caliber machine gun with one hand and twirl it over his head. His corporal's stripes were in recognition of his athletic prowess: He had only a fifth-grade education and had spent part of his growing-up years in reform school and in jail. When the days of the peacetime army had come to an end and the division had moved into the field, Targo had been put in charge of labor details.

Labor, in the field, meant mostly digging: latrines, sump pits, run-off ditches—there always seemed to be something else that had to be dug. Targo would throw a pick or a shovel at me and good-naturedly grin his head off: "Come on, professor, dig." Working with pick and shovel had not been part of my upbringing; it was not easy now.

Fortunately, I had the afternoon off. But there was always noise around, and it was not easy to find sleep. It was better when, after about six weeks, I was put on the graveyard shift. Then I got the morning off (and no longer had to take the general his shaving water), but the work details under Targo's watchful eye continued, only now they came in the afternoon and were followed by a strenuous physical training period. Col. François Eliscu was in charge. He wanted us not only in top physical shape but also prepared to meet the enemy at close range. He had us fighting one another with bayonets and knives, and if he saw anyone slacking off, he would come over and face the man himself. Every afternoon training period finished with a run up and down the steep walls of the gulches, ending almost always atop a sixty-foot tower, with only one way to go: down into the water.

About six weeks later, there came another change. I was moved to the meteorological section. The job of this small group was to measure air currents and densities at various altitudes by observing the movements of balloons and translate these into adjustment factors for artillery fire. Since the balloons had to be launched from open terrain, the "metro section" lived and worked about half a mile from our encampment in the gulch in a village of pineapple workers. Except for mealtime and duties like kitchen police and guard, the section lived a completely separate (and rather relaxed) existence. My mathematical training and particularly my ability to do simple computations in my head came in handy; the instruments the section used were relatively easy to learn, and I enjoyed the work.

Early on, when I was first attending the telephones in the command post, I discovered that the man on the line at the Thirteenth Field Artillery Battalion was my friend Sam Gilner. A few weeks later, each of us had his first opportunity to go on pass, and we decided to go into Honolulu together. But we found that the "entertainment" the city offered servicemen was not exactly to our liking. The next time we were eligible for passes we chose to go in the other direction and spent our time on the beach at Haleiwa, north of our respective locations. One subject that almost inevitably came up when we were together was what might have happened (or might happen in the future) to our OCS applications.

I spoke to the battery commander, Capt. Kenneth Deans, and he assured me that my application was still active and part of my file but that, for the present, the division was not sending anybody back to the States to go to school. I was too green to read between the lines, but before long everybody knew that our days on "the rock" were numbered, that the division was about to move to a new location. There was a lot of speculation about our destination. Would we, like the Twenty-fifth Division, be moved into combat at once? American troops were already in New Guinea and having a hard time of it. Perhaps that was where we were going. Eventually the rumor mill began to concentrate on Australia as our next stop. And Australia it was.

Camp Caves, Queensland, Australia

Soon we were shifted to a staging area for the impending move. Again my assignment was changed, this time to the survey section. But everyone was busy with the preparations for the move and, especially for lowly privates, it really did not matter what your assignment was; there was a lot of work to be done by everyone. There was excitement and eagerness in the air. Leaving "the rock" (where obviously the days of danger had long passed) meant that we would get that much nearer to the purpose for which we were in the army. Most everyone seemed to feel that the sooner we got into combat, the better.

We traveled to Australia aboard the *Mount Vernon*, the converted Matson liner *Lureline*. I do not know how many men were aboard, but I remember standing in line for two hours twice a day just to get meals. I was fortunate not to draw kitchen police duty; one of my cohorts who did reported that the feeding line was in operation from 6:00 A.M. to 6:00 P.M., with only an hour's break at noon.

After ten days at sea our ship sailed into Botany Bay, certainly one of the most beautiful sights in the world. We were loaded on busses that took us to our temporary housing at a racetrack north of the city. The trip through Sydney was unbelievable: people lined the streets and cheered, handing us flowers or throwing them as we went by. The Australians were obviously happy to see us. (We were the first major

American troop contingent to be brought in through the port of Sydney, and that may have had something to do with the tumultuous reception we received.)

The next morning we were told that everybody would be allowed to spend the day in the city but also that everyone had to be back at the racetrack by 10:00 P.M. Sam Gilner's unit was next to ours, and he and I agreed to do our sightseeing together, starting with the mandatory stop at the Hotel Australia, which, we had been told, had the longest bar in the world. In late afternoon we stopped at an out-of-the-way pub for a beer. Almost all the men in the pub were in their fifties or sixties; the younger men, they told us, had all been gone since the fall of 1939, and many of them had wound up in North Africa. One man said he had lost both his sons, and then he invited us to come to his home for dinner. We accepted and spent a pleasant evening with him and his small family.

The next morning, as the whistle called us out of our tents, the master sergeant in charge of the communications platoon was in front of the battery; the first sergeant was the only man in the unit who had not returned from the city. Ten names were called out, mine among them: We were to be ready to leave in an hour.

A train took us northward through Newcastle, Brisbane, and Bundaberg. By nightfall an army truck had dropped us off in a wooded area about fifteen miles inland from the town of Rockhampton, in northern Queensland. This was to be our training area, and our group was to clear the area and set up tents to receive the main body in a few days.

As soon as the division was settled in this area, named "Camp Caves," the Divarty survey section turned to its priority task: mapping the area in which the division would carry out its training and maneuvers. Except for the peaks nearest the coastline, there had been no mapping.

We now had an officer in charge, First Lieutenant Binckley, newly arrived from Fort Sill and a course in "advanced" artillery survey that had taught him that the first step in a mapping project was an aerial survey. But the two Piper Cubs we were to receive were still on their way from the U.S. The lieutenant probably made almost immediate friends of the entire section by inviting everybody to share in discussing possible alternatives. He asked about vehicles. All the equipment the division needed was being shipped, brand-new, from San Francisco. Sergeant Hatcher, our section chief, had heard that some trucks had arrived and were in a division pool. Could we borrow some? Hatcher volunteered to hunt down the warrant officer at the division pool who would eventually be our motor officer. An hour later the sergeant returned with a stocky man whom he introduced as Mr. Little. Lieutenant Binckley sent me to the mess tent for some coffee. When I returned everything was settled: Little would have three jeeps available the following morning; Hatcher would have the mess provide lunches for everybody going along. There was only one condition; Mr. Little wanted to drive one of the jeeps.

Lieutenant Binckley laid out a series of routes, all on wooded trails, with the intent of identifying site lines. We kept this up for over a week until our section's new equipment arrived. Then we went on weeklong schedules, measuring distances and angles, setting the exact location of every point needed to prepare a map. As one of the three privates in the section, my duties were to carry rods, run tapes, and clear lines of sight. But Lieutenant Binckley soon entrusted me with all the computational work that needed to be done. For the first time in Uncle Sam's army, I began to feel useful.

The four or five days each week in the field (or, as the Australians called it, the bush) were strenuous but enjoyable. The men in the section were congenial, and there was almost every day the opportunity to stop at one of the several "stations," farmhouses that were located at the edge of our training area. Often, as we stomped through the bush, we would flush out specimens of the unusual fauna that inhabits the Australian continent. We did not see many kangaroos; these huge but shy creatures would flee at the sound of our truck. But the smaller and much more graceful wallabies were almost like tame deer, so close would they allow us to come.

The weekends, of course, saw us back at our base camp, and, since the three privates in the survey section were unavailable at other times, each of us would always spend a weekend day on kitchen police. I did not particularly enjoy this assignment or the fact that it regularly came on Sunday, but one redeeming feature was that, by virtue of alphabetical order, my fellow "KP" was always Austin Flack.

Back when all of us had a day off in Sydney, the sergeants major of the four battalions and our first sergeant had gone to the city together, and, as I have mentioned before, neither our "topkick" nor the other four had been back on time. In fact, they still had not appeared when the main body of the division left Sydney for Rockhampton. When at last they showed up, duly escorted by members of the military police, General Lester gave them their choice: Given their rank, they were entitled to trial by court-martial; alternatively, he could simply strip them of their rank and reduce them to privates. In those days, "getting busted" was a simple and common procedure; similarly, promotions did not have to be one step at a time, and these five old soldiers knew that, once they had served as privates for, perhaps, six months, there was a good chance that their six stripes would be restored to them. They opted for reduction and, sensibly, were all transferred to other units.

Flack, a veteran of more than twenty years in the army who had been the sergeant major of the Sixty-third Field Artillery Battalion, was assigned to our unit. Our former first sergeant, Bullard, went to the Eleventh Field Artillery; our new one, John Harris, was also an old-timer who, because he had seen his first service with Pershing in Mexico, was known as "Black Jack" (Pershing's nickname in the army).

Every Sunday for four months Privates Flack and Heller peeled potatoes and scrubbed pots and pans together. In the process I picked up a great deal of the lore and the morale of the Regular Army. I never heard Flack complain. At the same time, he knew every shortcut to get the work done fastest and easiest. We were an incongruous pair, but we got along famously.[1]

The two other privates in the section had been promoted to private first class, and I was hoping that my turn would be next. But once again there came a change of duties (and in those days even the rank of "PFC" was tied to a scheduled position and not, as later became the rule, awarded mainly on the basis of time served). I was told to go back to the headquarters section, this time for duty as draftsman. I did not quite understand this since I knew that only one draftsman was authorized and that position was filled. In addition, there was absolutely nothing in

1. Sergeant Flack was back with the Twenty-fourth Division during the Korean war, was captured, and distinguished himself by his leadership under the conditions of the POW camp. In 1991, on the fiftieth anniversary of the attack on Pearl Harbor, he was given prominent attention as the only army survivor of the event still in the service, in the Old Soldiers' Home in Washington, D.C.

my background that might qualify me for the position. I said so to the first sergeant when he told me of the change. His answer was that he did not know what the score was but that the order had come from the general himself.

Once again, however, our unit was alerted for a move, and my first duties involved stenciling boxes for the files and other equipment of the command post. By contrast to the spaciousness and relative cleanliness of the *Mount Vernon* the ship we embarked on at Gladstone, a port city just south of Rockhampton, was a miserable tub, a Dutch freighter that had obviously seen better days. There were only two saltwater showers and no other onboard lavatory facilities, and the Indonesian crew's curried lamb was hanging in the open, adding to the pervasive odor of unwashed men. In addition, we had been put on Atabrine to protect us against malaria, and those not seasick were sick from the unaccustomed medicine. Several men became so weak that when we finally reached our destination, Goodenough Island off the eastern tip of New Guinea, they had to be carried ashore.

Goodenough Island and Hollandia, New Guinea

Forty-eight hours after our arrival at Goodenough Island I was back on a ship, but this time it was for a short trip only, to neighboring Ferguson Island. This was the training site of the Alamo Scouts, the southwest Pacific's equivalent of the Rangers. Forty men from our division had been sent there for six weeks' special training. A book published some years later asserted that all men who joined the Alamo Scouts were volunteers; I know I was there because I had been ordered.

It was about as demanding a period as I could imagine, let alone go through. There was a snapshot of me taken after I had completed Alamo Scouts training: my stepmother, to whom I sent it (but who did not save it) recalled that I looked "lean and mean." No wonder; we had been through jungle survival training, had qualified as parachutists, had spent two days in native canoes adrift on the sea, and had spent days with natives learning Pidgin English.

As our final exercise in the course, we parachuted on a dark night into the uninhabited part of an island, which, we were told, was held by the enemy, with instructions to explore the enemy's strength and location. The island turned out to be our own base of Goodenough, but half of our group were "captured" before they were able to realize that. Somehow, I managed to get through and was able to tag the division message center with a sign indicating that it had been "destroyed." The colonel in charge of the Alamo Scouts, as he dismissed us to return to our respective units, cited me as the outstanding student in the course.

I fully expected that, once returned to the division, I would be put on an advance scout team to be landed behind the Japanese lines. Instead I found myself at a drafting table. Two "war tents" had been set up for the planning of the next operation. The regular draftsman was in one tent, I in the other. I was severely admonished not to discuss my work with anyone outside our own war tent, and specifically not with the other draftsman. (The long-awaited PFC stripe came with this change in duties.)

At this time Allied forces had secured two major Japanese bases, Lae and Finschhafen, both in eastern New Guinea. The Japanese Eighteenth Army, estimated at 100,000 men, was centered at Wewak, about 350 miles west of Finschhafen. The planning group I was working for was preparing for a two-pronged landing near Hollandia (now called Djajapura), 225 miles to the west of Wewak. The code name for this leap of almost 600 miles was Operation Reckless. It seemed an appropriate label for the kind of distance involved.

It was not until a decade later, when I had become affiliated with the army's Command and General Staff College, that I appreciated the logistical complexities and the true recklessness of the plan. MacArthur's headquarters had resorted to a number of ruses to conceal its true intentions from the Japanese. One of them had the Twenty-fourth Division operate two parallel but totally separate planning efforts. In the other tent, where the regular draftsman was working, they were planning for an assault on Wewak. This, however, was a decoy. Counterintelligence had learned that during our stay in Australia, our draftsman had been drawn into a net of Australian Mafia types who, in turn, were being used by Japanese agents in Brisbane. That put him in a position to pass on a full decoy plan—this attack on Wewak. Whether that particular ploy worked was never known (it was only one of several stratagems used by intelligence to mislead the Japanese about our intentions), but it is a fact that the bulk of Japan's Eighteenth Army remained at Wewak and that the Japanese expected us to land there. Our draftsman was given "leave" to Australia just before the operation began and never returned to our unit. The incidental result for me was that I was now clearly the occupant of a position that called for two stripes (with a "T" below, indicating that it was a technician's rank and not a "real" corporal), and the promotion came along soon.

The attack on the aviation complex of Hollandia consisted of two prongs. The Forty-first Infantry Division landed at Humboldt Bay, east of the town of Hollandia, while our division went ashore at Tanamerah Bay to the west. Our artillery had been reinforced by two battalions of 155mm guns ("Long Toms") so that we would be able to support the advance with a total of seventy-two pieces. Our executive officer (Colonel Lang), the operations officer (Lt. Col. Taylor), the intelligence officer (Major Keating, newly promoted from captain), and most of the enlisted personnel of the headquarters were put ashore at the small village of Depapre; from there they were to coordinate the artillery support. General Lester, Lieutenant Early, another lieutenant who was newly assigned as assistant S-3, and the rest of headquarters' enlisted personnel, me included, had gone ashore about two miles to the east of Depapre, with the expectation that they would join the group at Depapre the next morning.

The landing was uneventful, but no sooner had we gone ashore than it became apparent that what the photo interpreters had identified as an exit road from our beach area was in fact an impassable swamp. When radio contact was established with Colonel Lang we learned that Depapre had turned out to be in a defile that effectively precluded radio communication with forward observers and liaison officers with the infantry. If there was going to be any kind of massive artillery preparation for next day's advance on the Hollandia airfields, it would have to be directed from our location.

Thus it came about that Brig. Gen. James A. Lester, most recently assistant commandant of the army's artillery school, and Technician Fifth Grade Francis Heller, lately a Ph.D. candidate at the University of Virginia, spent all night together bent over plotting boards and firing charts inside a blacked-out tent. None of the other enlisted men knew what needed to be done (and, to be sure, my knowledge came entirely from my nighttime reading in the command post in Hawaii); the assistant S-3 kept falling asleep and was finally sent away by the general (and promptly transferred out the next day). As dawn broke, Lieutenant Early (whom the general had sent to get some rest so that he would be available in the morning) came around to ask the general if he could bring him some breakfast from the field kitchen. The general replied, "Yes, and get some for Heller, too." As Early left the tent, the general put his arm around my shoulder and said, "Francis [he had never used my first name before], I am glad I had you with me tonight." A few weeks later, on his recommendation, I was awarded the Bronze Star Medal for that night's work. The citation said, in part, that I had performed "with the competence and skill of an experienced junior commissioned officer."

More important for me was that added responsibilities now came rapidly and with them promotions in rank. By early June I was promoted to the three stripes and two "rockers" of a technical sergeant and, because Master Sergeant Wallace had been granted leave to the States, I was the ranking noncommissioned officer in the headquarters, in charge of the operations platoon. But it would be another eighteen months before I learned that this was what "Jimmy" Lester and Colonel Kiefer had originally planned for me,[1] that I be the key enlisted man in division artillery when the Twenty-fourth hit the thick of the battle, the invasion of the Philippines.

How to get us from the swamp-locked Tanamerah Bay beach to the Hollandia airfields proved a challenge. The road from Depapre to the airfields was in such miserable condition that, once the airfields had been captured by the infantry, it was decided that all units with any kind of heavy equipment should go by water to Humboldt Bay and move to the airfields from that direction. The Forty-first Division, which had initially landed at Humboldt Bay, was already preparing for another operation (the seizure of the islands of Wadke and Biak, off the northwest coast of New Guinea); our division was to set up at the Hollandia airfields and move roadblocks into the interior to intercept elements of the Japanese Eighteenth Army as they attempted to escape from the trap into which MacArthur's leapfrog strategy had placed them at Wewak.

The road from Humboldt Bay was not in very good shape either, but army engineers had already begun to improve it. Even so, it took all day to cover the fifteen miles, and there were many stops along the way. At one point we were halted close to an abandoned Japanese army hospital which we promptly began to explore. Apparently, the Japanese had been totally surprised by our landings and had left in great

1. See chapter 4.

haste. I came on what had evidently been the quarters of a medical officer: There were medical books on a shelf; shaving gear and other toilet articles were laid out on a small table; two sets of uniforms were still hanging in a closet; and there was a fine pair of leather boots, which proved to be just my size. I promptly appropriated the boots as well as a pith helmet. Others did likewise: By the time we had completed our trip to the airfields, there was hardly a man who was not wearing some item of captured gear.

Our destination was a complex of airfields which the Japanese had built just north of Lake Sentani, an inland lake twenty miles long and four miles wide. North of the airfields, the terrain rose slowly until it reached a major mountain (Mount Cyclops) which protected the airfields and lake area from northerly winds. We set up a series of tent areas in the foothills.

Shortly afterward, army engineers began to build a headquarters area for MacArthur, his staff, and his family high up on the mountain. MacArthur was never popular with the troops in the southwest Pacific, and a contributing factor was this office complex in the jungle of New Guinea. Whether it was as elegant as rumor had it, I do not know. But we believed that an engineer company from our division was, for instance, diverted to build indoor plumbing for the complex at a time when the only facilities we had to wash (both our bodies and our clothes) were the brooks and rivers that came out of the mountain area. One of the trucks from our battery was used to carry a load of Persian rugs from the dock in Humboldt Bay to the general's private quarters.

But our own arrangements were not really uncomfortable. After the first week or so we slept in tents on cots with mosquito netting, and eventually we had a mess area with tables and benches. Army order was rather quickly reestablished. The beards most of us had grown quickly disappeared. The captured Japanese uniform items remained as souvenirs only or became barter material in moonlight deals with the navy and Seabees at Humboldt Bay.

As is good military practice, training resumed. But there were also logistical and tactical tasks. Supplies had to be unloaded at Humboldt Bay and, on a three-week rotation basis, one of our division's infantry battalions would be assigned to assist in that task. The Japanese were fleeing Wewak, and a battalion-size force, its members also rotating on a three-week schedule, was sent inland to set up ambushes along the enemy's escape routes.

I did not draw the stevedoring detail, but I recall two very different incidents that illustrate that duty. By virtue of my new rank and duties I now shared a tent with First Sergeant Harris and Master Sergeant McGlinchey, the communications chief. Once or twice a week the first sergeant would, without the knowledge of any of the officers, send a truck to the navy area at Humboldt Bay. It would leave loaded with assorted items of Japanese equipment that we had picked up on the way to, and in the clean-up operations around, the Hollandia airfields. It would return, always after dark, with various items of equipment and food from navy stores of the kind we usually did not see: eggs, frozen meat, once even real lettuce.

One night, after we had turned in, Corporal Becker, the supply clerk who was particularly adept at this barter trade, came into the tent and woke the first sergeant. He had, he said, brought back something extra special, but some work would have to be done on it quickly if we intended to keep it. We followed him to the truck and there, plainly visible in the moonlight, was an electric generator trailer, navy gray and with navy identification symbols.

In no time at all, "Black Jack" had assembled a working party that chipped away at the gray paint. There soon emerged the familiar olive drab army color. "Black Jack" let go with a stream of profanity, of which the mildest was "damn thieving gobs." Then the men working on the rear bumper called out: The bumper bore the marking "V-J"—our own unit identification: Becker had bought our own lost generator! "Black Jack" broke all records for known profanity. But "moonlight requisitioning" was common practice, encouraged by the (really unavoidable) fact that there was no property accountability in forward combat areas.[2]

My role in this episode had been strictly that of spectator, and so it was also in another event. Shortly after I had joined the Twenty-fourth Division in Hawaii I had run into Julian Mason (who had been a year ahead of me in law school at the University of Virginia). He was now

2. When we arrived in Japan in September 1945, our battery had two jeeps above authorization, and we went to great pains to conceal that fact for as long as we could.

a captain in the division judge advocate's office. I did not see him very often, but whenever I did he would tell me that, if at any time I got tired of my assignment in division artillery, he could easily arrange to have me transferred to legal work in the JA's office. A few weeks after we had come to Hollandia he had looked me up to tell me that his office had now been authorized a warrant officer, with the proviso that the person filling the position had to be educated in the law; all I had to do, Julian said, was put in for it, and the job, along with the higher rank, would be mine. I told him that I was quite happy where I was. Perhaps to whet my appetite he told me that there would be a general court-martial the next day and invited me to come and watch. I had never seen a military trial, so I spoke to General Lester, and he gave me the afternoon off to attend.

The accused was a young major, the executive officer of an infantry battalion that had been assigned to Humboldt Bay for stevedoring duties. While the unit was there, with the major in command, a Japanese plane had bombed the ammunition storage area, causing a major conflagration. The colonel in charge of the supply base had ordered the major to take his men and fight the fire and explosions. The major's response was that neither he nor his men were trained as firefighters, especially under such hazardous conditions. The colonel had repeated his order. The major remained adamant and was now on trial for refusing the lawful order of a superior officer.

Julian Mason was trial judge advocate (prosecutor). The division chemical officer was president of the board (military judges were not introduced until the Uniform Code of Military Justice went into effect in 1951). The defense counsel was a captain (not a lawyer) from the major's regiment. His plan of defense was simple: The order was so unreasonable that it could not qualify as a "lawful order." Mason's task was to argue that the colonel's rank and experience, taken together, put his order beyond dispute. In a microscopic way, it was a preview of the war crimes trials.

When the court recessed to deliberate on its judgment, the small audience was sharply divided. Yes, it had been a lawful order, but was it not beyond reason? When the court returned and announced its verdict of "guilty," a pall seemed to settle over the assembled spectators. The court then withdrew to deliberate on the sentence but returned rather quickly with its decision: A letter of reprimand would be placed in the major's file—nothing more.

Applause rippled through the audience. Friends gathered around the major. I walked over to Julian Mason who was beaming with relief: "I would have felt miserable," he told me, "if they had done any more to him." What had worried him, he said, was that it was common practice for courts-martial boards to hand down severe sentences so that the general who had to review and approve the findings could reduce the sentences, thus making him look benevolent. (Years later the colonel who had presided at this trial told me that in this case the much-maligned "command influence" had worked in the defendant's favor: The division commander, Maj. Gen. Frederick Irving, had told him before the trial that he hoped that the court's sentence would be no more than a reprimand. That reprimand was, on the same general's orders, soon afterward expunged.)

Julian again tried to talk me into seeking the warrant officer's position in his office. I told him again that I was quite satisfied where I was and did not wish to change. In fact, at about the same time I was offered the chance to go back to Australia and go through an officer candidate school that had been set up there. I declined that opportunity as well. The assignment I had, I thought and told Julian, was probably more important and involved more responsibility than the duties usually given to newly commissioned second lieutenants or administrative warrant officers.

Shortly after this had happened the first sergeant told the senior noncommissioned officers that our battery had received an order to furnish a senior NCO and twenty men to be part of a composite unit to "go inland." This was the first time that our battery had been called on for such duty. I told Sergeant Harris that I would go. He reminded me that, given my duty assignment, I would need to get the general's permission, but he acknowledged that it would solve his problem: He could not spare any of the sergeants in the communications platoon, and he did not think that Rudy Fox, the mild-mannered grocer from Leesburg, Virginia, who had just been promoted to staff sergeant in charge of the survey section was strong enough for the job. That left just him or me, and he did not have to tell me that he had just passed his fifty-fifth birthday.

General Lester was understanding. We were in the midst of refresher training, and that meant relatively light work for our headquarters. If I really wanted to go, he would approve. But, if this was the first sergeant's doing, he reminded me that it was very easy for him to say that he could not spare me, even for only three weeks. I told him that I felt the need to find out if I remembered what I had learned in the Alamo Scouts training camp. He smiled: Would I mind if he looked at my copies of the airmail edition of *Time* as the subscription came in and not wait until my return? I said I would tell the mail orderly to bring them to him. (By now, I had learned that he was interested in world news and appreciated seeing my copies of *Time* after I had finished reading them. Also by now, I had received, clearly at the general's suggestion, two packages with various "goodies" from Mrs. Lester, two more than I ever received from my family.)

Two days later a rather motley crew patched together from division headquarters and the signal, ordnance, and engineering units embarked on a small flotilla of amphibious trucks to cross Lake Sentani. From then on it was all on foot. Within an hour we were on a narrow trail through jungle so thick that the sun did not penetrate. Moisture hung heavy in the air; the ground underfoot was wet and slimy; the going was slow. We covered less than six miles that day but reached a clearing where a small tent area and a field kitchen, staffed by a small detachment of army cooks, awaited us. This was the first night's stop.

The following morning, clambering up a rocky streambed, we reached the top of the first, rather low mountain range. The air was clearer in this altitude and less oppressively humid, but it was still terribly hot. That night we strung our jungle hammocks along the edges of a clearing. The night air turned sharply cool; the sky was clear, the stars more brilliant than I had ever seen them.

Early the next morning we crossed another range and started the descent toward our destination. I was leading a squad of ten men, weapons at the ready since we now had to expect to run into snipers and enemy patrols. The trail had been marked by earlier ambush forces and at first passed through a wooded area that could have been in the lower regions of the Alps or the Appalachians.

Almost without warning we came upon a wide clearing. A small lake sat in a meadow full of wild orchids. About a dozen white deer stood in the shallow water, now attentively gazing in the direction of the intruders. I motioned the men behind me to stop as I absorbed the peaceful beauty of the sight. Then a familiar voice beside me said: "Some stupid son of a bitch is bound to start shooting." It was Corporal Targozinski, the old-timer who had supervised my early labor details when I had first come to the unit. But it did not take a shot: His voice was enough to scare the animals, which fled with graceful leaps. I was about to scold Targozinski when I saw the almost ecstatic expression on his face. "Professor," he said, using the nickname he had given me in those early days, "that's the most beautiful thing I ever saw." I certainly agreed.

As the day progressed and we descended further into the valley, we began to encounter indications of the enemy's presence. There were trails going from east to west, and occasionally pieces of Japanese equipment were scattered about. Then, suddenly, as we were about to enter another clearing, there were shots. The two men who were about ten feet in front of me went down, dead. I jumped behind a large tree as two Japanese soldiers came charging toward me, bayonets fixed. One of them, I think, yelled something like "Yank, you die." I fired my carbine; the one nearest to me went crashing down. I lunged forward and swung my carbine, stock first, at the other one. Trying to avoid the swing, he veered, and his momentum carried him past me. That gave me just enough time to pick up the dead man's rifle. Now I, too, had a bayonet fixed. It was none too soon: The Japanese had turned and was again rushing toward me. I parried his bayonet thrust (but probably forgot to give thanks for Colonel Eliscu's training). Now we were face to face. He smelled of sweat and olive oil. He kicked at me, aiming at the groin. I hit his knee with the rifle butt and jumped back. He came at me again and again I managed to divert his bayonet. Only this time I kicked, and he was not fast enough to catch my leg before it hit him across the shins. He stumbled and barely retained his balance. I took advantage of the opening, and my bayonet went into his side. But even as he fell he swung at me again. I used my bayonet a second time: The body in the brown uniform twitched convulsively and went dead.

I fell down exhausted. Seconds later Targozinski was by my side. He picked me up like a child and carried me back to the shelter of the trees. "Professor," he said, "you aren't just smart. You are one hell of a soldier."

I was breathing heavily, and my hands were shaking. It ran through my mind that I had *killed* two human beings.

Targozinski handed me his canteen. I had never seen such admiration on a man's face. The military police captain who was in command of our unit had come forward by this time. Targo pointed to the two Japanese bodies and told the captain that I had done this by myself and added: "But just last year, I had to teach him how to dig a ditch."

The remainder of our trek inland was rather uneventful. We occupied ambush locations that had been prepared by the units before us. Twice small groups of Japanese walked into the trap; each was quickly eliminated. We lost two more men and had several wounded. But our biggest problem was the high humidity. Most of us, me included, developed fungus infections, mostly on our feet but also on other parts of our anatomies. Our fatigues and canvas-topped jungle boots began to mold. By the time we returned to base three weeks later, half of us were barefoot, and all our fatigues were in tatters. How could the Japanese hope to escape?

Leyte, Philippine Islands

It was night before I dragged my tired self from the amphibious truck that had brought us across Lake Sentani to our battery area. A light in the orderly tent told me that the first sergeant was still at his table. I walked in on him, hoping that he might have some hot coffee on hand. He welcomed me with open arms, more cheerful than I had expected. As he filled my canteen cup with the hot brew, he gave me the big news: We had a new general! General Lester had been transferred to Fourteenth Corps, in the Solomon Islands. Our new commander was Brig. Gen. William Archbold.[1]

There had been two brothers in the army, both West Pointers, whom I will call Archbold. The older was a man of considerable ability, perhaps even brilliance. He died shortly before the United States entered World War II. William, the younger and our new commander, had served in the War Department while MacArthur was chief of staff of the army and, so his reputation ran, made up in "spit and polish" what he lacked in intelligence. Sergeant Harris had heard about him but, so he told me, had been ill-prepared when the new general had turned on him in the presence of his battery commander, criticized everything about the battery, and announced that he, the first sergeant, should expect frequent and demanding inspections.

1. Not his real name. I do not know what became of him.

Right now there was a problem that Sergeant Harris gladly dumped in my lap. There were only two typists in the headquarters. General Archbold and Captain Watkins, his senior aide and now our headquarter's adjutant, had given them the contents of two footlockers filled with orders and directives that General Archbold had issued in his previous command, which he wanted now to have retyped, with the only changes being the caption of each document and at the end the authenticating signature. (Nowadays we would feed all but the first and the last pages into the Xerox machine but, of course, no such thing existed in those days.)

Sergeant Harris alerted me that the two typists would intercept me before work the next day. They thought that it was just stupid to retype all the orders when it would not take very long to match them against the orders already in effect, identify those that had to be added or would replace existing orders because they differed, and type only those. The older one had told the first sergeant that he had mentioned this to Captain Watkins who, so I was told, "would not listen." So it was with some apprehension that I made my way from our tent area to the hut that served as the division artillery headquarters—and to my first encounter with Captain Watkins.

Colonel Lang saw me coming and met me outside the command post. In my absence the typists had taken their concerns to him and asked if some help could not be found for them; Lang had then talked to Watkins who had told him that the general had a very low tolerance for delay and was already demanding to know why *his* orders had not yet been distributed. Lang told me that Archbold's reputation was common knowledge among Regular Army officers; and he added that there had not been enough time yet to know where Watkins would fit in, that it was not unreasonable to assume that Archbold had placed him in the staff position in order to be informed about the attitude of the other officers.

This was the first time that I learned that Watkins was a lawyer. Lang thought this might make it easier for me than for him to get to know the new adjutant. He also told me that he and Watkins had agreed to stall on the typing problem until I came back and then let me figure out what could be done. By this time I had come to know Colonel Lang well enough that I could respond by reminding him that everybody knew that the first lesson new second lieutenants, fresh out of West Point, learned was "when in doubt, ask the sergeant!"

Then Lang took me over to Captain Watkins who was sitting bent over a table. At a mere five feet, six inches, I am used to being the shortest person in almost any group, but somehow I was not quite prepared for Watkins's height, a good foot more than mine. There was no other chair nearby, and the captain now stood, towering over me. Then he put one leg on the chair he had been sitting on and lowered his elbow to that knee. I would see him do that later on many occasions: it was an unobtrusive way of reducing his height advantage and putting shorter people at ease.

Had I heard about the problem with the retyping of the general's orders? With due respect, I asked if the captain had perhaps advised the general that there would be some delay, and why? Watkins did not bat an eye: "I know General Archbold well enough to know that he would be angry and displeased." In that case, I suggested, it might be best if I did not present myself to the general until I found a solution to our problem. Watkins did not change expression; yes, he agreed, that would be best. Then, remembering that his previous job had been as General Archbold's personal aide and that he was not a "regular," I added that unless the captain wished to be informed, I did not intend to let anyone know where I found the necessary typing assistance. There was a glimmer of a smile in Watkins's eye. But it was not until long after General Archbold had departed that Watkins asked me where I had finally found help. By this time he knew, of course (as he had not on the day we met), that I too was a U.Va. lawyer, and so he had guessed that I had gone to the judge advocate's office; he was amused when I told him that my help had come from the division chaplain's office.

Even after General Archbold had been relieved (and sent back to the States accompanied by an army psychiatrist and two armed guards), Bill Watkins never talked about his days as Archbold's aide. But we could also see how Archbold treated his junior (and remaining) aide, Lt. "Rollo" Nash. We could see how he demeaned the staff officers. Everyone in our battery knew that the first of its members killed was not the victim of a Japanese bullet but was shot by General Archbold, who had come storming out of his tent in the middle of the night, screaming that he was being attacked by Japanese snipers and wildy firing his pistol into the air. He fatally wounded the switchboard operator on duty.

Watkins was never heard to say a bad word about Archbold and that in the face of the increasingly hostile attitude toward Archbold among the other staff officers. I saw most of them in later years—some while I was back on active duty during the Korean War, some of them while they attended the army's Command and General Staff College at Fort Leavenworth just an hour's drive from where I live. Without exception, they were full of admiration for the stable, sensible way Bill handled what might have been a trying situation for others. I remember just one occasion when he allowed me to glean what his thinking was. By this time I had been given a direct commission and, even though there is still a huge gulf between a second lieutenant and a major, it is nothing compared to the distance between even a high-ranking NCO and an officer. This was just before Bill was due to return to the States. We had been talking about the "era Archbold" and this (roughly) was Watkin's comment: "You know, I had two silver bars [a captain's insignia] and you had five stripes on each arm [a technical sergeant's]; but that one star of his [a general's] could beat us every time."

Once Watkins knew that I was a fellow Virginia lawyer, he and I struck up a friendship that lasted well beyond the war years.[2] He soon confirmed what most of us had quickly suspected: General Archbold had only one aim in this war, and that was to come out of it a greater hero than his brother might ever have been.

Artillery generals are, as a rule, not in a good position for heroics. General Archbold was determined to make his opportunities. We were now in the planning stages for Operation King Five, the invasion of Leyte, the first stage in MacArthur's promised return to the Philippines. Somehow Archbold managed to persuade the division planners that "his" artillery should be well forward, so much so that it would be necessary for a small detachment from division artillery headquarters to land with the first wave of infantry assault troops.

Lieutenant Nusbaum, the assistant operations officer, would lead the small team. I was to accompany him, along with a radio operator and one man with a submachine gun. Targozinski volunteered to be that man.

Our task was to locate an area on the beach where a command post could be dug in for General Archbold. A later wave was to bring in, along with two squads of the communications platoon, ten men who were to

2. Watkins died in 1999 after a highly successful legal career in his home state of South Carolina.

do the excavation job. This would enable our general to be ashore and functioning in his headquarters well before the division commander could do so.

I had done the drafting of the maps and diagrams that went with the artillery's part of the attack plan. This was going to be vastly different from the brief and relatively painless Hollandia operation. Red Beach Two, where the Twenty-fourth Infantry Division was scheduled to go ashore, was dominated by a large hill, identified on our maps only as "Hill 522," which, according to intelligence reports, was full of mortar and machine gun positions. The intelligence element's estimate was that "moderate" resistance could be expected on the beach itself. Naval gunfire would neutralize Hill 522, though it was noted that (1) the Japanese had tunneled deeply into the hill and might be difficult to dislodge, (2) the reverse slope of the hill could accommodate enemy artillery in positions where it could fire on the beach area, and (3) only a portion of our own artillery would be able to reach the other side of Hill 522.

"A-day" for the landing on Leyte was October 20, 1944.[3] Lieutenant Nusbaum's detail had been placed with a platoon of the Nineteenth Infantry for the landing operation. Shortly after daybreak we were on deck and began to climb over the side of the transport ship into an LCT, a small landing craft. The navy was already shelling the beach. As I clambered down the heavy netting I missed a step and, to avoid falling, I twisted my left arm through the ropes. My watch strap broke, and my government-issued wristwatch disappeared into the water. It did not seem like a good omen.

The landing craft pushed away from the transport and began to move in circles, waiting for the signal to pull into formation and move toward the beach. An infantryman next to me was fingering a rosary. I wished I had brought one myself and began silently to say the prayers, using my knuckles as if they were beads.

A flare went up, and the small boats moved into line. Our craft was the fourth or fifth from the left flank, but, as we came closer to shore, the rough water made for uneven progress, and we were at the extreme left flank when the landing craft finally hit bottom. The coxswain called out "Ramp down," and the young infantry lieutenant yelled, "Let's

3. "D" was never used in MacArthur's command.

go." By prearrangement the four of us from division artillery were to be the last off.

The water was waist-high; we were a good fifty yards from shore. The infantrymen were moving as fast as they could. Bullets were spewing out from a clump of trees on the beach. Suddenly, Lieutenant Nusbaum, about ten feet in front of me, fell backward. The water around him turned red: He had been hit squarely in the chest. I could hear Targo behind me: "The bastards got him! Run, professor, let's get out of the fucking water!" I needed no encouragement: Seconds later I lay, panting, on the edge of the water, Targozinski and Scaglione, the radio operator, on either side of me.

"What the hell do we do now?" asked Targo. I told him we would do what our team had been assigned to do: Move to the center of the landing area and spot a place for the command post. "If the yellow bastards will let us get out of here," was his rejoinder. This was, indeed, a good point. Evidently only about half of the infantry platoon had made it past the slight rise of the beach just in front of us. I told Targo that we had to get to the top of that rise to find out what we were facing. Slowly, hugging the sand, we inched our way upward.

The sand ended about thirty feet on the other side of the rise. Scattered palm trees, most of them with their crowns shot away by the navy's shelling or the Japanese counterfire, were interspersed with clumps of low bushes and tall grass. The infantry had pushed about 150 feet in. Their .30–caliber machine gun was protecting the left flank of the skirmish line (which, of course, was also the left flank of the entire Red Beach landing force). To the right, another platoon had moved ahead by about another two hundred feet. Enemy fire came from close in. Several of the infantrymen in front of us went down; the rest, hardly more than a dozen, seemed to be frozen to the ground. (As I was soon to find out, one of those killed had been the lieutenant leading the platoon; the platoon sergeant had been hit before he even got ashore.)

A burst of enemy fire hit the machine gun crew. It looked as if both of them had been killed (in fact, one was only blinded and survived). We could see brown-clad figures moving in the direction of the machine gun. If the gun were to be turned against us, the infantry on our right would be attacked from its rear as well as its front. I do not remember what I thought or whether I thought at all. I simply yelled at Targo:

"Let's get that machine gun!" and started for it. He, with his strength, size, and athletic ability, got there before I did and started firing our machine gun at about eight Japanese who were no more than fifty feet away. I grabbed Targo's submachine gun. Between the two of us we got them all.

I looked around: we were too far away from our own troops and too exposed. Targo picked up the machine gun, and I told him to move it to a group of trees where we would be able to protect the platoon to the right and in front of us. No sooner were we set up than another squad of Japanese came rushing at us, bayonets fixed, from the left. A voice behind me called out "caro mio." Scaglione, the radio operator, had been crawling forward to join us, and a shell had hit the heavy radio pack he carried on his back. But he made it to our position and the three of us managed to beat back the attackers.

Since my watch had fallen into the water, and neither of the other two carried a watch, I did not know how much time had elapsed, so I was greatly relieved when I saw that a new wave of our own troops was moving up and past me. An officer crouched next to me: "Are you A Company?" he asked. "No," I said, "I am with Divarty." "What the hell are you doing here," he came back, "and where is A Company?" "The first platoon is pretty well gone," I said, pointing at the bodies to our left, "but I think the rest of the company is just ahead of us." He still wanted to know what I was doing there. I told him briefly and asked him to have some of his men take over the machine gun position we held so that the three of us could turn to our assignment. (That same captain later filed a report saying that, by holding the machine gun position, we had saved the remainder of A Company and possibly the entire first battalion and recommending that I be given the Congressional Medal of Honor. Eventually I was awarded a Silver Star Medal. I always thought it was too much for doing something that, at the time, seemed to me just obvious.)

Now that we had turned over the machine gun, the three of us made our way toward the center of the landing area. It was soon evident that, as the landing crafts' approach pattern had been disrupted, the left flank was widely extended while there was a veritable traffic jam the closer we came to the center. Scaglione was the first one to spot our follow-up group. Staff Sgt. Al Jungblut, the wire sergeant, was delighted to see me: He had to start on some wire lines, but, as the only NCO present, his orders also were to stay with the command post excavation project until relieved. I told Targozinski (who, after all, was a corporal) to take charge of the digging and told Jungblut to take his linemen and get going on his job.

I did not know some of the men who were digging. A group of replacements had been assigned to our unit just before we left Hollandia but after I had gone to my ship for the trip to Leyte. Jungblut had told me that half of the digging crew were from among these new arrivals and that it seemed that they came "from the bottom of the barrel." Several looked to be near the upper age limit (forty-two) for the draft. Nobody wore rank insignia, and thus I assumed that the older man who stood watching the whole scene as if it did not concern him was one of the replacements. I picked up a shovel and threw it at him. I suspect that I probably said something like "get your lazy ass down there and start digging." Whatever it was, he gave me a surprised look but took the shovel, climbed into the hole, and started to dig. About a half hour later a young officer came hurrying along and asked if anyone had seen General Blanchard. The man I had sent digging called out of the hole: "Here I am, John." Before I could say anything, he turned to me and said: "Sergeant, you did exactly what you should have done. I had no business being here and I am glad you put me to work." He asked for my name and unit and walked off with his young aide.

Not much later General Archbold arrived. He was furious that the command post was not ready and seemed to take it as a personal affront that Lieutenant Nusbaum had been killed. By this time Al Jungblut had managed to get a phone hooked up with a liaison officer with the infantry, and soon there was a report that the infantry had secured the Palo-Tacloban Highway, which was about two thousand yards inland from the beach. At once, our general ordered the command post moved a half a mile further inland. We had managed to get set up but only partly dug in by the time it got dark.

The general ordered his personal tent surrounded by two feet of sandbags and a double circle of trip wires. He was, he announced, the prime target for Japanese infiltrators and had to be protected at all costs. It was a procedure that would be repeated whenever we were in proximity of the enemy.

As a matter of fact, several Japanese snipers were in the trees even as we set up the command post, and two of our men were wounded that evening. No shots ever came close to General Archbold, but, as I mentioned earlier, once he came charging out of his tent, wearing only his underwear, and proceeded to fire his .45 wildly into the air, with fatal result to one of our men.

There were only two tents set up, the general's and the command post tent. Colonel Lang, Colonel Taylor, Major Keating, and I, as well as one or two other enlisted men spent our nights in the command post: higher headquarters wanted all sorts of reports as of midnight. As Taylor said he had anticipated, our 105mm howitzers were too close to Hill 522 to shoot over it and too close to the infantry in front of 522 to support the attack on that obstacle. The Eleventh Field Artillery's 155mm howitzers, with their higher trajectory, were able to hit the reverse side of 522 but essentially, thanks to General Archbold's eagerness to be well forward, our artillery was virtually useless in these first few days.

On the other hand, the artillery pieces were prime targets for the Japanese. On several occasions, always at night, our headquarters would receive reports from firing units that they were under direct attack from enemy parties. We would then call the navy liaison officer in the division's operations section and request "star shells," low-level illumination bursts, from navy guns. This would enable the gun crews to see the attackers and mount an effective defense.

Such a call came on the third night around 11:00 P.M. from the Thirteenth Field Artillery. Colonel Taylor told me to put in the request for star shells. But the navy liaison officer at division headquarters, a lieutenant commander at the other end of the line, said he was sorry but the navy could not oblige! On the contrary, he said, his instructions were to advise the ground units to prepare for bombardment by enemy naval vessels. Our navy had pulled out to meet some major Japanese fleet units, and there was a danger that other Japanese ships would move in close enough to shell our positions on shore.

We had been without air cover throughout and had been told that none could be expected until the fourth or fifth day. Jack O'Grady, the young sergeant from San Luis Obispo who had succeeded Thomas as the second-ranking NCO in our headquarters, said he did not mind getting killed, but he wanted it to be a fair fight. Colonel Lang settled us down by calmly challenging me to a game of chess.

For some reason the Japanese attack on the Thirteenth's perimeter came to a halt. The night became eerily quiet. Then, from a distance, came the dull sound of naval guns. We were awaiting, though we did not know it, the outcome of the crucial naval battle of Leyte Gulf.

We still had not been shelled when dawn broke, and shortly afterward our infantry took Hill 522. The road to the interior was now open. And, as we moved through the little town of Palo later that day, there was the most welcome sight of all: The planes overhead were unmistakably ours. At last we would have air support.

As we moved north through towns named Alang-alang and Jaro, General Archbold was fuming: The ground on either side of the only road was too soft to carry the load of the howitzers and trucks; there was no alternative road. He could not move the artillery any faster than the infantry was advancing and, thus, could not position the guns where they could fire point-blank at the enemy.

At the same time we were already suffering casualties. Capt. John Brady, the senior of our two pilots, was lost on a reconnaissance mission, which he had flown against his professional judgment when the general ordered him up at a time of day when we knew that Japanese planes would be operating over our area. "Pancho" Mendez, a delightful fellow from Monterey whom I had gotten to know well during our stay in Australia (he was the instrument operator for the survey section) was literally blown apart by a land mine. Al Jungblut, the wire section chief, was invalided back to the States with a nervous breakdown after he brought his driver, Victor Vieira, back from an ambush with his head blown open. Art Siegwalt, a veteran of World War I, lost both legs in the same encounter. And those men were not the only ones.

The advance had begun to slow when the Japanese brought in two crack divisions from China. The new troops had arrived through the port city of Ormoc on the west side of the island. This counterforce met our troops at a point that came to be known as "Breakneck Ridge" and stopped them there. By this time we were again without air support, partly because of the distance between our lines and the bases from which the planes would have to come, partly because the support aviation had been diverted to other operations. Our infantry was stopped, as was everything behind it, including General Archbold and his artillery.

Our unit halted just west of the small town of Carigara, with our four battalions just ahead of us and some heavier guns, part of the artillery of the Tenth Corps, right behind us. General Archbold was frustrated beyond description. If the corps artillery was firing, he would come storming out of his tent and demand that "his" guns should be heard. He would arbitrarily select targets from the map and order Colonel Taylor to have all our guns fire on them. Since he often picked targets that were too close for the safety of our own lines, Taylor set up a system by which he would give the battalions the general's specified targets while I, on another telephone line, would pass on a code word that meant "fire at the time ordered but ignore the target designations and fire where you know it is safe to do so." I do not know how many rounds were wasted in this manner, but it happened virtually every night and often lasted for a half hour or longer.

Later, after General Archbold had been sent back to the States, Colonel Taylor explained to me why Archbold seemed to be so totally in error in his plans for our artillery. The Germans, he told me, had been able to overrun most of Western Europe in 1940 because their war planners had recognized that the tactics of the First World War had been costly and to little avail. Instead of fortified lines there had to be rapid movement, and the instruction at their tactical schools was appropriately changed.

The American service schools were using the American Civil War as the model for future action. What General Archbold had learned was that the best use for artillery was in point-blank fire on the enemy. But when Taylor and Colonel Lang had attended the basic artillery course, a completely different model was used, in a change developed by the school's assistant commandant, then none other than our own Jimmy Lester. Artillery guns were to be used in support, not in place, of the infantry. The newer weapons developed since World War I could fire longer and higher and, most important, with greater accuracy. Archbold's direct action approach was a relic.

What made the situation more difficult for those of us serving under General Archbold was the man's irrational personal behavior. As we were halted near Carigara he insisted that the troops be brought up to "spit-and-polish" standards in both personal appearance and the maintenance of equipment. Since we were, literally, knee-deep in mud, this was impossible. But the general would hold inspections, often without advance notice, and berate soldiers in the ranks if their fatigues were dirty. Since none of us enlisted men had any change of clothing, the only laundry facility was a nearby muddy creek, and the daytime temperature was usually in the high nineties, there was simply no way to have clean clothing. One's best hope was for a heavy downpour when we would strip off our clothing, get soaped up, and let the rain rinse us off. The fatigues would get the same treatment and, of course, they had to be put back on soaking wet.

Archbold's outbursts against the officers of his staff (and no one was immune) were as unpredictable as they were humiliating. At last Lang and Taylor sought an appointment with the division commander (by this time Major General Woodruff). As a result the inspector general was ordered to visit all units under General Archbold's command. A routine part of any such inspection was that time would be set aside when anyone could see the inspector general and register whatever complaints he might have. In our battery alone, the inspector general heard complaints for eight solid hours, and every one of the officers and most of the enlisted men went to see him. General Archbold never moved out of his tent while this was going on, but he had positioned himself in such a fashion that he could see all who went to the inspector general, and I could see him write down their names.

I knew the inspector general's chief clerk fairly well, and he told me later that the file of complaints from our battery alone ran to nearly four hundred pages. But nothing happened. General Archbold, meanwhile, was spending his time preparing recommendations for awards for himself. He called Lang and Taylor in and ordered them to sign documents he had drawn up and typed nominating himself for both the Distinguished Service Medal and the Distinguished Service Cross, the highest awards in the army after the Congressional Medal of Honor. It says something about the overall state of morale that both complied.

Major General Irving had been relieved as division commander when repeated efforts to overcome the Japanese resistance at Breakneck Ridge failed. Irving was well liked by the troops, and there was widespread feeling that he had been made the "fall guy" for poor planning at the corps level.[4] Irving's successor, Gen. Roscoe "Spike" Woodruff, was a member of West Point's famous class of 1915 (Eisenhower,

4. Irving lived past 100 and, almost to his death, was annually honored at West Point as its oldest survivor of World War II.

Bradley, etc.); he had also been the starting center on army's football team. His orders from the Tenth Corps commander, Maj. Gen. Frederick Sibert, were to clear Breakneck Ridge and open the road to Ormoc. To do this he decided to execute two flanking maneuvers (called end runs on the football field): The second battalion of the Nineteenth Infantry would move through the hills to the left (east) of our lines; the first battalion of the Thirty-fourth Infantry would do the same on the right (west) flank.

It all happened very quickly. The higher-ups had made it clear that they wanted prompt results. The infantry threw in everybody available, including cooks and clerks. Everyone was to be ready within hours. The artillery was expected to provide a liaison officer (usually a captain) and three forward observers for each battalion, each of them with an instrument operator and a radio man. But the ranks of junior officers had been severely depleted during the preceding combat action, and the two artillery battalions involved, the Thirteenth and the Sixty-third, asked for help from division artillery. Colonel Taylor, who was well aware of the stress that General Archbold's behavior had created in our headquarters, asked me if I wanted to go out as a forward observer. His assumption, he told me, was that it would take massive concentrations of artillery fire to prevent the Japanese from reinforcing their positions at Breakneck Ridge. I was familiar with the procedures for this kind of fire coordination and could be of more use with the forward troops than someone who had mainly worked with pinpoint use of artillery support. I would not be the only noncommissioned officer forward observer. A few other ranking officers were also being assigned to serve as forward observers with the two infantry units.

I did not hesitate. I was placed on detached service with the first battalion of the Thirty-fourth Infantry, with instructions to channel all requests for artillery support through division artillery. Once again Steve Targozinski volunteered to go with me, and so did Scaglione, the radio operator who had been with us on the day of the landing. The date was November 10, 1944.

Within a couple of hours the three of us had reported to the first battalion of the thirty-fourth infantry and found ourselves on a landing craft that took us about thirty miles up the coast. It was from there that we started our trek to a hill mass identified on the map as Kilay Ridge, just south and west of Breakneck Ridge. On the map it appeared to be about two days' march. Unfortunately the map proved highly inaccurate: Anything beyond the coastal areas had been entered not on the basis of land surveys but as reported by untrained native informants.

We reached our first day's stop only to discover that the supplies that were to await us there had not arrived: There was no food for us that evening or the next day. (A party of Filipino bearers caught up with us later and brought us rations and additional ammunition.) Finally, after four grueling days spent making our way through incredibly rugged terrain our Filipino guide proudly announced that we had reached our goal. I was with the lead company at the time as was the battalion commander, Lt. Col. Thomas "Jock" Clifford. One thing was immediately apparent: The Japanese had also recognized the importance of Kilay Ridge; in all directions, they had dug ditches, evidently to serve as a fall-back position if they were forced back from Breakneck Ridge. The crest was composed of jutting rocks, with heavy forestation beginning about 150 to 200 feet farther down. All around us there appeared to be nothing but wooded terrain with the exception of a deep ravine to our left that allowed a view of a road. With my field glasses I could see a few Japanese trucks slowly moving northward.

The colonel called for the artillery forward observer. I moved to his side and reported: "Sir, Sergeant Heller." "Good God," he said, "are we all out of officers?" I had prepared a reply: "Sir, I am here to report for duty as FO, on order of Colonel Livingston Taylor." (I knew that Clifford and Taylor had been classmates at West Point.) "Well, sergeant," he said, "if Livvy trusts you, I will too. Now get on your damned radio and see if you can figure out where the hell we are. There is to be some sort of checkpoint that you red-legs have shot in that is supposed to give us our position." I knew what he was talking about. Just south of Breakneck Ridge was (or had been) a road bridge that served as the artillery base point for the whole area. Every gun in the division had been adjusted by firing on Concentration 42.[5] I knew that this was where I had to start.

"Duke 3, this is Duke 34," Scaglione started to call. After about five

5. Each battery had established what settings would produce a hit on a registered target, in this case concentration forty-two. A forward observer would report what adjustments the guns would need; the fire direction center would convert these into settings; a minimum of hits resulted in an "effective registration."

calls I could hear Colonel Taylor's voice: "Duke 34, this is Duke 3. Professor [we had agreed to use Targozinski's nickname for me on the radio], are you on the objective?" "Affirmative, Blackie," I replied, using his code name. "Request Concentration 42." "Roger, wait." After a minute or so, he reported: "One round, Concentration 42, on the way." I waited. There was no sound nor any sign of smoke. I asked for another round, with the same result.

"What the hell is going on?" asked Colonel Clifford. It seemed to me, I said, that we might be further south than we had expected to be. "But this *is* Kilay Ridge," the colonel insisted. I suggested that while we were on Kilay Ridge, it could be that Kilay Ridge was not where the map showed it to be. "Maybe I'd better call the liaison officer up here," Clifford said, implying, of course, that a captain might know better what to do than a mere sergeant. I could feel Targozinski, next to me, bristle. The radio came alive again with Taylor's voice: "Professor, do you want to go on?" "Affirmative. Concentration 42, south 2,000, request smoke."[6] Targozinski mumbled: "What are you shooting for, Ormoc City?" "No," I said, "I just want to be sure I get one I can see." "On the way." This was Jack O'Grady's voice. I counted the seconds. Then, slowly, to our left and about half a mile away, the white smoke of a phosphorus shell rose out of the woods. "Wait," I said into the radio. "Have you got it?" Clifford asked. "Yes," I said, "no need to call the captain."

Targozinski had already set up the aiming circle.[7] I oriented the instrument, then I called for a repetition of the previous fire. When the smoke came up, I took a reading of the angle from north (we called this an azimuth). Then I asked for another round but another one thousand yards further south and measured its azimuth. I gave both measurements to Colonel Taylor and in a matter of seconds he gave me, in code, the coordinates of our location: Kilay Ridge was over three miles south of its map location. We were not at the enemy's flank; we were well behind his lines.

We stayed on Kilay Ridge for twenty-two days. By the third day the Japanese had discovered our presence and begun to attack our position two

6. Two thousand was change in ranges; "smoke" the type of ammunition to be used. Changes in direction, like those in range, would be given in yards.

7. A portable instrument used to measure directions (an azimuth) from magnetic north.

or three times a day. Once they succeeded in pushing us off the ridge, but we were able to recapture it. B Company was effectively cut off from the battalion for much of the time. The situation became increasingly precarious. We began to run low on ammunition and rations. The weather was miserable. It rained almost daily. The rocks became slippery and slimy, the ground between them turned into knee-deep mud. The army's official history relates that at about this time the commander of the Thirty-second Division (which had relieved the Twenty-fourth at Breakneck Ridge) radioed to Clifford: "You and your men have not been forgotten. You are the talk of the island, and perhaps the United States. Army beat Notre Dame 59 to 0, the worst defeat on record."[8]

Clifford was everywhere. He was cheerleader, first aid man, chaplain (nearly one-fourth of our 565 men became casualties); he was a living example of the best kind of leadership.[9] Occasionally, during breaks in the weather, a light plane would fly over and drop us supplies, but half the time the containers came down too far away for us to retrieve. At one point we went without food for thirty-six hours, with only rainwater to relieve the situation.

The one fortunate development was that the Japanese mortars cut down many of the trees in front of us. As a result we were now able to see a much more extended stretch of the Ormoc road, possibly as much as two miles or more. Because the captain, liaison officer, and one of the FO's, a second lieutenant, had been wounded and evacuated, the remaining FO (an enlisted man, Staff Sgt. Jack Jablonsky, who had also come out of "that" battery at Fort Bragg) and I took turns getting the guns zeroed in on the road and calling for fire whenever we saw traffic.

It was my turn to observe the road when the radio came alive: "Duke 34 or 36, this is Duke 3. Do you hear me?" "This is 34," I replied. "I hear you four-by-four." That meant that I could hear but not too well. "Professor," it was Livvy Taylor, "how is observation?" "Fair," I reported. "Listen carefully," Taylor said. "Four-zero [that was the liaison plane] reports a large convoy of trucks and weapons moving north. They are

8. M. H. Cannon, *The War in the Pacific: Leyte, the Return to the Philippines* (Washington, Government Printing Office, 1954), 234n.

9. For another testimonial to Clifford's leadership, see John F. Shortal, *Forged by Fire: General Robert L. Eichelberger and the Pacific War* (Columbia: University of South Carolina Press, 1987), 79–80.

approximately ten miles south of the stretch you can see. Four-zero had to return to base. Can you control fire from there? Over." "Affirmative," I answered. "We will give you everything we got, including corps. Ask for a check adjustment, and then we will shoot the works on your command. Do you have that? Over." "Affirmative, Blackie." "Allow ninety seconds to TOT [time on target]."[10] "Roger. Anything else?" "Negative except, if we pull this one off, we'll have them licked."

"What's going on?" It was Colonel Clifford who had come up to my position. I told him what Taylor's instructions were. "Well, damn it," was his comeback, "don't waste your time yakking at me. Do your stuff."

I got back on the radio. "Duke 3," I said, "this is 34. Fire mission. Over." "34, this is 3." This was O'Grady again; Taylor would be busy on other lines coordinating the battalions of artillery that would respond to me. "We are ready for your fire mission." "Registration. Concentration 101 [that was the center of the stretch of road I could see], one round, HE [high explosive], fire when ready." In a matter of seconds came the report: "On the way." I could see the impact: It was slightly over the target. I called in the necessary corrections: It came in short. The third round was exactly where it was supposed to be: We had an effective registration; that is, we were ready for the massive bombardment. "34," this was O'Grady again, "Blackie will call you when we are ready." I acknowledged and waited. It was Targozinski who broke the silence: "Jesus, how much stuff are they going to shoot?" I had not even figured that yet. It would depend on what kinds of guns corps artillery could put in. I knew they had two battalions of "Long Toms" (155mm guns) close to our own gun positions, so at least sixty guns would be firing. (In fact, there were ninety.) I suddenly realized that, on my command, an overwhelming mass of steel and explosives would be unleashed. I asked Targo if he had his rosary with him. He reached for his first aid pouch: "Since that day on the beach, I always keep my beads in here." He handed me the rosary and joined me as I said one period of the prayers.

Scaglione had been monitoring the radio. "Sergeant," he called, "Colonel Taylor calling." I took the receiver: "Duke 3, this is Three-four.

10. TOT meant that a multiple number of guns would hit the same target (or target area) at the same time.

Over." "This is Blackie. We are ready, Francis." I could not remember that he had ever used my first name before; Regular Army officers just did not address noncoms that way. "How is observation? Over." "Five by five," I reported. "Francis," he went on, "Tommy [that was Colonel Lang] and I know that you are the guy who will pull this off. Just tell us when you want fire. We will give you one salvo, one battery. If necessary, give us an adjustment. If not, your command 'repeat fire' will give you the TOT. We can repeat the TOT for eighteen minutes running if necessary. If you want the fire moved along the road, give us the adjustment. Do you have any questions? Over." "Negative on questions," I replied. "Affirmative on instructions. Will proceed. Stand by. Over."

"Jesus, Maria, and Joseph!" That was Targozinski at my elbow. "Son of a bitch, what a ringside seat for the fireworks!" That was Colonel Clifford standing behind me. I had my field glasses trained on the road. A few vehicles had come into sight, moving slowly around the holes that previous shelling had produced. I waited until the lead truck was just short of Concentration 101. By now, a good part of the column was in view. I could make out about a dozen tanks and some twenty-odd truck-drawn guns.

"Fire mission," I said into the radio. "Concentration 101, battery one round, H-E, fire when ready." O'Grady acknowledged. Almost at once he reported "on the way." I had figured from the tables I carried that it would take about fourteen seconds for the rounds to land and silently counted. As I reached "fourteen," four rounds landed, almost squarely on 101. Two trucks appeared to have been hit; the column came to a halt. "Repeat fire," I said.

This time it took nearly a minute and a half but then the valley exploded. I consulted my tables while the firing continued. Then I ordered a shift that moved the center of the fire a quarter of a mile down the road. The guns continued to pour it on while I ordered further shifts that covered the road for two miles up and down. At last it seemed that all movement had come to an end. "Cease fire," I said. "Mission accomplished. Estimate over one hundred trucks, tanks, and artillery destroyed. Over." "Three-four, this is Three. Blackie speaking. Well done. Over." "Give me that radio," Clifford said. "Livvy, this is Jock. Your boy up here did one hell of a job. You can just leave him with me for the duration." "No way, Jock," came the reply, "we need him here. Jock, we'll send up an L-4 [the technical name for the observation plane] to assess the situation. Panther Six [that was the Thirty-second Division commander] is here with us. You will get his orders through us. Over."

About a quarter of an hour later we could see the spotter plane flying down the valley. I tried to pick him up on my radio, but either he was transmitting on a frequency I did not have or he was observing radio silence. Colonel Clifford had stretched out on the ground near me and had fallen asleep. I suddenly realized that I, too, was dead tired. None of us, of course, had more than catnapped since arriving on the ridge.

The radio came alive. Taylor asked for Clifford. I woke him up and handed him the receiver. The pilot had confirmed the damage estimate. What few vehicles were still moving had turned around and gone south. Our infantry at Breakneck Ridge would attack within the hour. If they succeeded in cracking the Japanese positions at Breakneck Ridge, the Kilay Ridge detachment's mission would be over. Jock Clifford broke into a loud cheer and shared the good news with the men in our vicinity.

Our little team—Targo, Scaglioni, and I—began to prepare for the trip down from the ridge. Scaglioni, who had hardly said anything since we started on our assignment, surprised me: "Sergeant, I hadn't prayed since I left St. Margaret's grade school in Scranton, but when you asked Targo for the beads, I knew that was what I needed. That got me thinking about something else Sister Hildegard kept telling us, that America is a mix of people. And here we are: I am a spick, Targo is a bohunk, and you have just got off the boat. . . . " (Years later, Targo still recalled these words.) "We are all Americans." "But he," I pointed at the exhausted Clifford, "he *is* America."

The attack on Breakneck Ridge was successful, and the next morning the First Battalion, Thirty-fourth Infantry, soon to be known as "the lost battalion of the Pacific,"[11] more than a hundred of its men wounded, began the long trek down. Fortunately, about halfway down, we were met by some Filipino scouts and a party of doctors and

11. That designation has also been claimed by the Second Battalion of the Nineteenth Infantry, the other part of Woodruff's pincers movement. Actually it was more deserving of the title than our unit: Once I had established our location, we were not "lost," but 2/19 never was able to fix its place in the jungle mountains and was, indeed, lost.

stretcher-bearers. The Twenty-fourth's assistant division commander, Brig. Gen. Kenneth Cramer, was with them. He embraced Colonel Clifford like a long-lost son and told him that the battalion was being recommended for a Presidential Unit Citation. Then he reached into his pocket, pulled out a set of full colonel's eagles, and pinned them on Clifford, who tried to wave them off. The citation, he said, was appropriate: There had been 565 heroes on Kilay Ridge; but he should not be singled out. If anyone deserved something special, it should be Sergeant Heller. "Without him, we would still be sitting up there waiting for the next *Banzai* charge." Targozinski's booming voice broke in: "You are damned right, Colonel!" There was no doubt who he was cheering for.

I spent about a week in a field hospital, both to regain my strength and to cure the festering sores that ringworms and fungus had caused all over my legs and lower body. Colonel Lang and Colonel Taylor came to visit me, Taylor beaming as if I were his favorite pupil. Jock Clifford, he told me, was recommending me for the Distinguished Service Cross. My reply was that I just hoped that I would be able to wear the citation badge, if in fact the battalion was to receive a citation (and eventually it did, and I was included). If anyone deserved a DSC, it was clearly Clifford himself, and if there was anything I could do to help bring that about, I would be most happy to do it. (Jock Clifford was awarded the DSC, but it came too late. He was killed in action on Mindanao a few months later, before the award had been made.)

Mindora and Mindanao, Philippine Islands

What had happened while I was gone from our base? Was General Archbold still with us? Oddly enough, in all my radio contacts with Divarty headquarters, neither his name nor his code designation had ever been mentioned. Colonel Lang said that he was and that things were continuing to deteriorate. The inspector general's report had been sidetracked at higher headquarters. Lang and others had persuaded the division chaplain to report the dismal state of morale in Archbold's command through his channels. If that did not work, they really did not know what to do. Paul Keating had nearly broken under the steady stream of abuse from the general, and Lang had arranged for Keating to be transferred to the States. His place as S-2 had been taken by Maj. Max Pitney, the executive officer of the Fifty-second Field Artillery Battalion.

More important, the division was in the process of moving to another island, Mindoro, but our headquarters would be among the last elements to make the move. Thus, there would be a time span when General Archbold would have only our battery on which to vent his spleen.

When the time came for us to join the rest of the division on Mindoro, our staff and the headquarters' enlisted men made the move by air, in a C-47 (the military designation for the DC-3). General Archbold made it clear that we owed this preferred treatment to his connections in high places. He did not seem to miss an opportunity to let us know just how well he knew General MacArthur. On a few occasions he would add that he knew that we were all against him but that we would never "get him."

It did indeed begin to look that way. Colonel Lang told me that the reply the division chaplain had received from the chief of chaplains at MacArthur's headquarters was an order to stay out of the whole affair. The division chaplain had, however, also spoken to General Woodruff and had related to Lang that the division commander was deeply concerned about the situation.

Eventually, after we had moved to Mindoro, General Woodruff persuaded General Archbold that his annual medical examination was overdue. To this end, Archbold would fly to Leyte where, so he told Lang and Taylor, he intended to tell General MacArthur with what a group of disloyal officers he had to contend.

Two or three days later, shortly before the evening meal, I was alone in the command post tent when General Woodruff walked in. He had earned the nickname "Spike" as an All-American football center at West Point; not only was he built like a powerful line player, he also had the blunt manner to go with his appearance.

Who would be on evening and night duty in our command post this day, he wanted to know. When I told him that it would be one of the clerk typists, he told me to change that. "Stay at ease," he said. "I have heard a lot about you, sergeant. I want you here tonight. Now keep this strictly to yourself: The doctors at the General Hospital on Leyte did what I hoped they would do. They are sending General Archbold back to the States for psychiatric evaluation. They think he might turn violent: There will be a doctor and two guards going back with him. He is back here now to pick up his personal belongings, but I don't want him to take any papers out of here. If he tries to take *anything*, I am giving you a direct order to prevent it, by force if necessary. Do you have a .45 [the standard army pistol carried by officers and ranking noncommissioned officers]?" "Yes, sir," I replied. "Wear it," the general said, "loaded. The chief of staff [Col. Hugh Cort] has already gone and removed the firing pin from General Archbold's pistol. I don't want to take any chances. By the way, Colonel Cort will take over here tomorrow morning. You will find him a very different kind of commander." He turned as he left the tent: "You look like you ought to see a medic yourself, sergeant, and I don't mean a shrink. Are you feeling all right?" I thanked him for his concern and told him I was feeling fine. In fact I was running a fever and feeling lousy.

When a two-star general tells you to be prepared to point your pistol at a one-star general, you know that the situation has become dire. Even though General Woodruff had told me to keep the matter to myself, I told Lang and Taylor about his visit and the orders he had given me. They had already been told about the change in command that was about to happen and were delighted. To be sure, Hugh Cort was not a West Pointer. He had gone to OCS in World War I and then stayed in the army, but he enjoyed the reputation of a highly competent and fair officer. Colonel Taylor observed that I looked under the weather and offered to spend the night in the CP in my place. I declined the offer: General Woodruff had given his order to *me*.

But General Archbold never showed up, and I know not what ever became of him. By early next morning he was gone. At 8:00 A.M. Col. Hugh Cort walked into the command post tent, shook hands with all the officers and men present, and said that he looked forward to working with us. At noon, he walked to the mess area, insisted on going through the line, and then sat on the ground with some of the enlisted men to eat his first meal as the Twenty-fourth Division Artillery commander.

Unfortunately I did not have an immediate opportunity to enjoy the improvement in morale. There was obviously something wrong with me. For several days I tried to doctor myself with aspirin from the aidman attached to our battery until he flatly told me that I was a fool not to go on sick call. When I did, Major D'Elia, the doctor, told me I might have pneumonia and sent me to the hospital. There I was diagnosed as a case of infectious hepatitis and put in a ward full of nothing but jaundice patients.

I could not remember how long it had been since I had been in a bed. In any case I was too sick to enjoy it. I was seriously ill for about a week. Then improvement started to set in. Colonel Lang came by and brought me fresh fruit that he had collected on a trip to the interior of the island. He also told me that the division was alerted for another operation. He wanted to know if I would be out in time. The nurse on duty doubted it. I implored him not to leave me behind. The way the army in the southwest Pacific worked in those days, if you were left behind after your unit moved, you became a "casual" and were likely to be sent anywhere. Colonel Lang said he would see what could be worked out.

Another visitor was a complete surprise to me: my brother Tom. He had just arrived on Leyte as a replacement. While waiting for his assignment, he had found out that most of the Twenty-fourth Division was now on Mindoro. He had hitched a plane ride to come and see me. The battery mail clerk had brought him to the hospital.

I had last seen Tom on the day our parents arrived in New York in the spring of 1941. I knew that he had been drafted in late 1943, but no more. He told me now that after basic training he had been assigned as a chaplain's assistant in a camp in California where he had met and married a girl who was now working (and waiting for him) in San Francisco. Once the war was over, that was where he wanted to settle down.

Tom also had news of Steve, our youngest brother. There had been cryptic references to Steve's whereabouts in our stepmother's occasional letters. Tom now told me that Steve had availed himself of an option extended by the British government to persons interned as enemy aliens (as Steve, because of his German passport, had been classified) to volunteer for army service as "sappers" (engineer troops). Steve had wound up in North Africa with a mine-clearing unit. Not only did he survive this hazardous duty, but he acquitted himself so well that he was sent back to England for officer training. Though technically still an enemy alien, he was now an officer with a tank unit in Montgomery's army.

Tom and I had a good visit. After he returned to Leyte, he was assigned to the Ninety-sixth Infantry Division and participated in the invasion of Okinawa. He was wounded on the first day and returned to the States. Although he later became a professional army officer and rose to the rank of colonel, that one day on Okinawa was all the hostile fire he ever experienced.

A few days later Colonel Lang came in again. He sat down on my bed and talked very low. He had figured out how to get me out of the hospital, but it was all against regulations and I was not to breathe a word to anyone. He had reconnoitered the area and found that there was a gap in the chicken-wire fence that surrounded the hospital. This afternoon, while I was out for exercise, I should go and look at the place. Tomorrow, at 4:00 P.M. exactly, our message-center jeep would drive by that hole in the fence and pick me up.

It went like clockwork the next afternoon. Sergeant Gumerus was there on the dot. A set of fatigues and a helmet were in the jeep, and by the time we reached the main road my hospital garb was out of sight and, except for the hospital slippers on my feet, I looked like the technical sergeant I was.

But when we reached the battery area I realized that I was still very weak. I could barely walk the distance from the jeep to the tent I shared with the first sergeant. Gumerus called Corporal Marks, the aidman; I began to fear that I would soon be on my way back to the hospital. But Marks obviously had his instructions. He took a blood sample as well as my temperature and told me to drink often from the pitcher of fresh pineapple juice he put next to my cot. About a half hour later he returned with some pills with instructions from Major D'Elia to take two every six hours. But he did not want to see me. I was, after all, absent without leave from the hospital and, as a medical officer, he could not be a party to the caper Colonel Lang had arranged. (Strictly speaking, I suppose, I am still AWOL from the United States Army 165th Station Hospital.)

The operation we were scheduled for was to take us to Mindanao. There a combined force of marines and the army's Forty-first Infantry Division had just landed at Zamboanga, a major port at the southern tip of western Mindanao, the southernmost Philippine island. Our division was slated to go ashore near Panang, on the eastern shore of Moro Gulf (the body of water between eastern and western Mindanao). From there we were to cut across the island and capture Davao, the second largest city in the Philippines.

We embarked at Mindoro on April 10. I was still rather weak, but Colonel Lang arranged it so that I could go aboard without having to carry my own belongings. Fortunately the sea was calm, and the combination of sunshine and sea air did much to speed my recovery. It was a far cry from that miserable boat ride from Australia to Goodenough Island!

It was on the third day at sea that the announcement came over the public address system: "Now hear this. It has just been announced in Washington that President Roosevelt has died. Repeat: The president is dead. That is all." The flag on the main mast was slowly lowered to half-staff.

FDR dead—it was hard to believe. Someone asked me: "Who is President now?" I could not remember. Under a special act of Congress we had all been able to vote in the presidential election in 1944, and I had voted for FDR and his running mate, but who *was* that running mate? After a while I recalled the name Truman and that he was a senator from Missouri. But who was he? And what would it mean that he was now the president?[1]

FDR *was* America. And now he was gone. But for me he was more than a distant figure. I remembered hearing him give the commencement address at the University of Virginia in 1940: Italy had just joined Hitler in the war against France, and Roosevelt had scathing words for Mussolini. I recalled seeing him in an easy chair in his son's living room in Charlottesville (FDR Jr. had been a year ahead of me in law school), laughing uproariously as he entertained the small group of law students his son had assembled, presumably to serve as entertainment for his illustrious father. I saw myself with FDR Jr. in the Oval Room of the White House and the president's flash of recognition: "Oh, yes, you are the young Austrian who collects stamps. Let me show you some of my collection," and my awe as he proceeded to do just that—the president of the United States showing his stamps to a twenty-three-year-old nobody who was not even a citizen. The others might think only that the president had died. For me FDR was more than that; he had touched me directly and so did his death.

Two days later we went ashore at Panang. There was no resistance, but we knew that more than 30,000 Japanese (the Thirty-fifth Army Corps) were still in eastern Mindanao. The map showed that we were on Highway No. 1, the "Sayre Highway." It might have qualified as a slightly improved cow trail back in the States. On the second day a group of Filipino irregulars came out of the hills with their leader, the almost legendary Colonel Fertig, an American engineer who had long lived in the Philippines and after the Japanese invasion assumed the leadership of the guerillas in eastern Mindanao. His followers called Fertig "general," but rumor had it that he had assumed that title on his own initiative and that MacArthur had refused to deal with him until he agreed to accept a commission as a lieutenant colonel. A slightly different account

1. Thirty years later I told this story to Hawaii's Senator Daniel Inouye (the prototype for Capt. Shigeno Sakayama in James Michener's epic novel *Hawaii*) and he said that the same thing had happened to him in Italy where he served with the 442nd Combat Team, the famous unit of Nisei volunteers. He could tell his men who was now president.

of Fertig's demotion appears in William B. Breuer's *MacArthur's Undercover War.*[2] The same book also contains a photograph of Fertig as he appeared when he joined us: Breuer describes him as an "eccentric," and he looked the part. Because General Woodruff's and General Cramer's tents were not up yet Colonel Fertig was received in Colonel Cort's tent; thus, I was able to overhear some of the conversation between our generals and the guerrilla leader. General Woodruff asked Fertig how long it had been before he had made contact with General MacArthur's headquarters. Colonel Fertig laughed uproariously. When, after weeks of trying, radio contact had at last been established, he had asked for "ammo and more ammo." The next day a plane had indeed dropped three boxes: One contained a mimeograph machine while the other two held paper to feed it.

We followed the highway toward the east coast of the island, but we saw only a single Japanese "Zero." We passed imposing fortifications on the hills on both sides of the road, but their heavy coastal guns were all pointing east. Our attack from the west made them totally useless, especially without enemy planes in the air.

We reached the east coast, some twenty miles below Davao, after about ten days, with only minor delays caused by small Japanese units that sought to slow our advance by roadblocks and ambushes. There was more resistance at the edge of Davao, but it, too, vanished quickly. The enemy faded into the plains area that surrounded the city and the hills beyond.

We set up camp on Talome Beach, just short of the city. Within a few days we were sleeping on cots and in tents. A volleyball court and a shower unit soon followed. There was an air of unreality about it: We would get into our vehicles in the morning, after a hot breakfast, and literally "ride forth to the wars," five to ten miles inland, and be back in the afternoon in time for a shower, a game of volleyball, a (green Australian) beer or two, and a movie after dinner.

It was after a day thus spent in the forward area that Sergeant Wallace (who had recently returned from his extended leave to the States) told me that the division artillery commander wished to see me in his tent after dinner. When I reported to Colonel Cort, Colonels Lang and

2. Breuer's account was published by John Wiley & Sons in 1995. See 84-85.

Taylor were there, and so were Major Pitney and Bill Watkins (himself recently promoted to major). Colonel Cort was serious: "Sergeant, I have observed you and I have received reports from others about you. I have concluded that you are in the wrong place." What was this about? Was I about to be transferred, but why and whereto? The colonel continued: "I want you to be back here at 7:30 tomorrow morning. Major Watkins has prepared all the necessary papers and he will then swear you in as a second lieutenant, field artillery. Congratulations, Lieutenant!" He grinned broadly as I stood dumbfounded. Lang, Taylor, Pitney, and Watkins each shook my hand. The phone rang; Colonel Cort lifted the receiver; the call was for me. "Mister," it was Jock Clifford, "it's about time. I have been telling Hugh Cort for months that you are the best damn artillery lieutenant I have ever seen running around with sergeant's stripes! Come on out and join me for some fun." (He would be dead two weeks later, but I never had any doubt that it was his word, more than anything else, that brought me this unusual advancement [usually called a "battlefield commission"].)[3]

I went back to our tent area in a daze. There was a small group of men in front of the tent I shared with Carmel Wallace and "Black Jack" Harris. As I came close, the first sergeant called out "Attention!" and they all saluted. Colonel Lang had told him just before dinner, and he had told the others while I was with Colonel Cort. I was deeply moved. These were the men I had lived with for over two years: "Targo" and Scaglione, Jack O'Grady, Carmel Wallace, Rudy Fox. . . . We had shared so much. They asked me what job I would have as an officer. I realized that I had not asked that question and had not been told.

I found out the next morning that there was something else that I had not been told. When I went to his tent, Hugh Cort was wearing the single star of a brigadier general. As a general officer, he explained, he was entitled to two aides, and I would be designated as his aide. But the assistant S-2/survey officer, Captain Ford,[4] had just left to attend a naval

3. This suspicion was confirmed when I learned, a few days later, that Jack Jablonsky, the other sergeant forward observer with the "lost battalion" and, like myself, a product of the "OCS battery" at Fort Bragg, had also received a battlefield commission. Obviously, only Clifford would have had reason to recommend both of us at the same time.

4. Lieutenant Binckley came down with Dengue fever on Leyte and was sent back to the U.S. for extended hospitalization.

gunfire control school, and I would therefore temporarily be in charge of the survey section.

But first, he said, he had a special job for me. He showed me a set of aerial photographs on his work table. Our front line was indicated in blue crayon. Red markings identified Japanese positions. He pointed to a yellow circle halfway between the blue line and the cluster of red marks. "The infantry has not been able to get over this ridge, and we have not been able to give them support because we have not been able to get any observation on the Japs. The tree here," he pointed to the yellow circle, "looks like it is tall enough to give us the observation we need. But it is about two hundred feet in front of our lines. The infantry has tried five times to get there, without success. I figure that a small team [of] eight or ten men might make it." He turned to face me: "I would not *order* anyone to do it but I think you could do it. Will you try it?" I did not hesitate. "Yes, sir," I said. "What other men will I have to go with me?" "Francis," he said, his arm around my shoulder, "I mean it: It's strictly a volunteer job. See if some of your old friends will go with you but make it strictly voluntary, you understand?" That made it serious for me.

I asked "Black Jack" to call the men of the battery together and then I explained my mission. I told them that we would be on our own in advance of our lines and that there was no telling whether we could reach our objective. And I stressed that this was strictly voluntary. I had hardly finished when Targozinski called out: "I am with you, professor, ah, sir!" And then the hands went up, one after another, even the cooks' and the supply clerk's, until I had my choice of the whole outfit. In later years I have often reflected that no one ever did me a greater honor than did these men, some of whom had known me as an awkward recruit and all of whom had seen me, until just a few hours ago, as one of them.

We set out that evening and spent the night with the forward company of the Nineteenth Infantry. At daybreak we crossed our lines and began our move across no-man's-land toward our objective. I led the way, partly crawling, partly in a low, crouching walk. We were within fifty feet of the huge tree when the Japanese discovered us and opened up with a couple of machine guns. Two of the men were hit, fortunately not seriously. I motioned the others to follow me as I circled to get the tree between us and the enemy. We lay still for about ten minutes, then I passed the word that we would move to the tree one at a time. Targo said he wanted to go first. I told him that we needed someone who would make a small target, and there was no one shorter than I.

We made it to the tree. Targo helped me get up on a heavy branch about ten feet above the ground. General Cort was right: the position provided full view of the Japanese entrenchments. I called for artillery fire. An hour later our infantry was able to reach what had been the enemy lines. My little squad, carrying the two wounded men, returned to the camp area on the beach. General Cort offered me a shot of Scotch, the first drink of regular liquor I had had since that day in Sydney so many months ago.

For the next several weeks I performed a miscellany of tasks. Captain Ford was taken ill at the navy school and did not return. Thus, on some days I would go out with the survey section. But as the Japanese withdrew further and further into the hills, there was little opportunity for coordinated artillery support and, hence, little need for the kind of survey operations that our unit normally provided.

On some days I would spend hours in a rather unique observation tower that was part of a hemp factory in a small town just south of our beach position. From there one could see the entire slope of Mount Apo, a volcano of nearly 10,000 feet and the highest mountain in Mindanao, which towers over the Davao plains area. Some of the Japanese units had moved up and had tunneled into the flanks of the mountain, and we were, rather systematically, searching them out. The tower allowed us to direct artillery fire over most of the area. As Livvy Taylor put it, it was like shooting fish in a barrel.

On other days I functioned as the general's aide and accompanied him on visits to the artillery battalions. One day we flew in our two small liaison planes across the island to Cotabato for a formal call on the *datu* of the region. On July 4, all three of the division's generals went into Davao where a parade was held to celebrate the city's liberation. Afterward the governor of the province had an informal luncheon for the generals, their staff officers, and their aides. There were some young women present, in native gala dresses, and after lunch there was some dancing. It had been over three years since I had danced.

I had had one weekend pass while I was at Fort Bragg, three three-day passes in Hawaii, a one-day leave after our arrival in Australia—twelve days in thirty-three months. Previously I noted that the men I served with were eager to get into combat; what I did not say was that there was behind that sentiment the all-pervading realization that the war we fought, unlike that in Europe, offered no respite. We knew that, if we survived, we would not get to surroundings that even resembled home until the fighting had come to end.

Few accounts of the war years acknowledge how different the war in the Pacific was from the war in Europe. A rare exception among historians, David M. Kennedy wrote that

> [t]he Pacific was a peculiarly alien place for American servicemen, and an achingly lonely one too. Most of the fighting took place in the tropics, home to exotic diseases like dengue fever and filiarisis, a lymphatic infection. Malaria was so endemic throughout the Pacific islands that troops on the ground were put on a compulsory regimen of Atabrine, a drug of dubious efficiency which the men resisted because it jaundiced the skin and was rumored to cause insanity and impotence. For the moment, impotence was in any case a small worry, since there were few available women, as evidenced by the fact that servicemen in the Pacific had markedly lower rates of venereal disease, the traditional soldier's scourge, than did those in Europe; AWOL (Absent Without Leave) were also lower in the Pacific, because there was no place to go. So was the incidence of death and wounding, since most casualties were inflicted by artillery and mortar shelling, for which the Japanese were not well equipped. The standard Japanese infantry rifle was also of such inferior design that it forced Japanese soldiers into close-quarters fighting, for which they kept their bayonets fixed at all time. Unlike their comrades in Europe, who typically fought long campaigns against modern, mechanized German adversaries, fighting usually at rifle-shot length and beyond, the American soldiers and Marines in the Pacific experienced long ocean crossings and brief bursts of combat, much of it in harrowing hand-to-hand struggle with poorly outfitted but ferociously motivated Japanese imperial soldiers.[5]

Davao was the nearest thing to a city we had seen since Rockhampton (which was nothing to write home about), and Davao was a shambles. (The main course at the governor's Fourth of July gala was water buffalo steak, incredibly tough and totally tasteless.)

5. David M. Kennedy, *Freedom from Fear: The American People in Depression and War, 1929–1945* (New York: Oxford University Press, 1999), 813–14.

Very few of us received mail on any frequent basis. My stepmother wrote about once a month, mostly complaining about the close quarters they lived in and the need to have ration cards to buy sugar. My copy of the airmail edition of *Time* came to me as a gift from Harry Clemons, the university librarian back in Charlottesville. That was the extent of my mail call. Others had even less. We never saw a war correspondent; Red Cross workers were, apparently, only in the larger (and therefore rear-area) hospitals. If you were in a unit in the southwest Pacific area, you were there for good and felt largely forgotten. Our battery clown, a regular by the name of Cheek (with the unlikely first name of "General" which used to get him into constant troubles back in Hawaii) came up with a song to which the refrain went "Two more months in the jungle and I'll be an honorary ape." There were times when that did not sound funny.

Nobody ever talked about the next phase of the war: We took it for granted that the Japanese would fight to the bitter end. We had encountered them at close range; there could be no doubting that we would have to fight them on their home soil and that they would resist fiercely.

Under deep secrecy our division had, on orders from MacArthur's headquarters, begun to plan for its assignment during the invasion of Japan. The whole thing was so hush-hush that only a few selected officers were allowed inside a carefully concealed and equally carefully guarded war tent; what limited drafting and drawing needed to be done was intrusted to me alone. The maps I worked on were of the Tokyo-Yokohama area. This was Operation Coronet, and the Twenty-fourth was one of four divisions scheduled to make the initial assault. What was scary was that MacArthur's master plan assumed that these four attack divisions would be wiped out within the first seventy-two hours of the invasion!

The news of the dropping of the atomic bomb on Hiroshima came to us like most news did—garbled and piecemeal. It was hard to understand. Col. Dwight Beach, our new executive officer (both Lang and Taylor had returned to the United States in late July), tried to explain it to us. He had a master's degree in physics, but I had difficulty following him. What was clear was that here was a weapon of unprecedented power and that its use might well mean the end of the war and with that the cancellation of Operation Coronet. The Twenty-fourth Division would not be doomed on the beaches of Japan.[6]

6. While I was on occupation duty in Japan, "Coronet" was carried out as a command post exercise (i.e., without troops). But to make it less cut-and-dried, each troop unit was represented by one American soldier, accompanied by a Japanese behind the sign identifying the advance elements of the Twenty-fourth Division Artillery. Suddenly the clouds that had obscured Mount Fuji parted to reveal that huge dominant mountain, I could not help but feel that, but for the atomic bomb, this is where I would have died. In later years I shared this experience with my friend Alonzo Hamby, and he included it, though somewhat garbled, in his magisterial biography of President Truman, *Man of the People: A Life of Harry S. Truman* (1995), 337.

Okayama and Himeji, Japan

Word of Japan's surrender reached our outfit while most of us were watching an evening movie. I went back to our tent area to spread the good news. Colonel Beach was in his tent, reading. His reaction surprised me; dejectedly, he said, "Now I'll never make general." (In fact, when he retired from the army in the early sixties, he wore not one star but the four stars of a full general.) Camp had turned noisy. Since beer was distributed only once a week and this was not one of those days, many of the eruptions were expressions of doubt.

Fighting did not stop at once. The Japanese forces on Mindanao were out of communications with their own higher headquarters, and not until mid-September did General Tomoshika, the commander of their Thirty-fifth Corps, enter our lines to surrender. Some Japanese units on Mindanao never gave up. Forty years later some of their survivors were reported to be still living in the mountains, cohabitating with the natives.

I (and others) now faced the question of whether to go home or go to Japan. Shortly after the end of the war in Europe the army had announced a point system for the return to the States of personnel overseas and the release of some of them. It was a combination of time in the service, time overseas, and time in combat, plus points for battle credits and combat decorations received. There was one qualifying number for enlisted men and another, higher, number for officers. As an enlisted man I would have been eligible for immediate return to the States, and most of my friends—Targo[1] and "Black Jack" Harris among them—had left in June and July. As an officer I would become eligible for return in September. Should I go home?

Home, of course, was Charlottesville, though in fact I had been in the Twenty-fourth Infantry Division almost as long as I had lived in Virginia. And what would I do there? Eleanor was married to another; my good friend Father Louis Rowen was dead. By contrast, if I signed on to stay in the service somewhat longer, I could not only get to see Japan but have a rather interesting assignment. General Cort had been designated to command a separate task force, which was made up of the Twenty-first Infantry Regiment, the Fifty-second Field Artillery Battalion, and some smaller supporting units. While the main body of the division would serve as the occupation force on the island of Shikoku, Task Force Cort would proceed to the city of Okayama, on Honshu, and handle the occupation of three prefectures, Okayama, Shimane, and Tottori. General Cort had chosen another second lieutenant to be his second aide and told me that he would use me more as a staff secretary. It sounded interesting; I opted to stay in the army until June 30, 1947.

It was all very orderly. In Manila, GIs had rioted to be sent home, but we had no such activities, mainly because fighting continued. We were also off the main routes and had to wait for shipping. Eventually our convoy arrived in Kure harbor in the western part of the island of Honshu. We were the last component of the American occupation forces to land in Japan, possibly also because our area was considered less critical than others. Even though Kure and its environs had been occupied for a month (by the Forty-first Infantry Division), we went ashore in full battle gear, steel helmets on our heads and ammunition in our weapons. By contrast, the Tenth Corps staff officers meeting us were decked out in "pinks and greens," the garrison uniform that officers with desk jobs then wore in the States, and sentries were standing post without the steel part of helmets, just as they would back home.

1. I was able to persuade General Cort (and with him General Woodruff who had the appointing authority) to send Targo home with a Bronze Star Medal.

General Cort's first stop was at Tenth Corps headquarters, where he reported to the corps commander, Major General Sibert. The corps had taken over the buildings used by the Japanese naval command for the Inland Sea, an imposing compound on a hill overlooking the city. Kure itself was only partially destroyed. Both the general and I were struck by the quiet manner of the people and the almost complete absence of any women or children in the streets. Our escort officer from corps headquarters explained that, prior to the arrival of the occupation forces, the government had admonished citizens to behave properly so as to give the Americans no excuse for excessive action against the civilian population. Subordinate officials, including those in Kure, had elaborated on this admonition by specific references to the danger that American soldiers would routinely seek to rape Japanese females and abuse Japanese children.

Some of Kure's more prosperous districts had remained undamaged, and it was in a villa in one of these districts that General Cort and his immediate staff were temporarily housed. To my surprise there was a full Japanese staff on hand, and two bottles of "Suntory" whiskey were on the table in the main room prepared for the general. He and his two aides had an excellent dinner in his suite and retired early.

The next morning a major from Tenth Corps arrived with a U.S. army staff car and took the general and me to see Hiroshima, a relatively short distance from Kure. Although it had been two months since the first atomic bomb had been detonated over the city, what we saw was still a vast wasteland with few signs of life. The surviving population had settled in a ring of makeshift dwellings, most of them a combination of cardboard and corrugated metal sheets, around the outskirts of the city. Here, even more than in Kure, the people seemed intent on ignoring us; most of them scurried along silently with their heads down, their eyes averted. Indeed, if there was one thing that struck me about Hiroshima, it was the overwhelming quiet befitting a huge graveyard.

On our return to Kure we found a Japanese official in morning coat and striped trousers awaiting us. He introduced himself as Mr. Ito, the Japanese liaison officer assigned to our headquarters. The Japanese government had drawn on its diplomatic corps to staff the prefectural governorships and the liaison offices with the occupation forces. Ito had served in the embassy in Rio de Janeiro and in the consulate general in Chicago. His English, while accented, was excellent. His job, he explained, would be to provide liaison between General Cort and the governors of the three prefectures that made up our zone of occupation.

The city of Okayama, so Mr. Ito reported, was ready to receive us the following day. Our advance party, headed by Max Pitney (who had been promoted to lieutenant colonel after General Cort reassigned him from our headquarters to command the Fifty-second Field Artillery Battalion), had already prepared a billeting plan for the troops but had not yet selected quarters for the general; there were, said Mr. Ito, several possibilities, and Pitney had thought it best to leave the choice to the general.

We traveled from Kure to Okayama by train, on a route that, for the most part, hugged the mountainside. Between the train tracks and the seashore there was barely enough room for a narrow road which my map identified as Highway No. 1. It rained for much of the time, but the view out on the Inland Sea, with its countless small islands, many of them with graceful *torii* arches, was entrancing. I was not surprised when the general started whistling a tune from *Madama Butterfly*.

For about the last half hour the train's route moved away from the seashore and across a flat, open area. Several industrial installations were visible. The land was heavily cultivated, and we could see men and women busily working in the fields. The city of Okayama, we knew, had been heavily damaged in a fire raid in June. As our train approached, the picture was not much different from that we had seen in Hiroshima: There were large aggregations of shack dwellings at the outskirts, then a vast area where nothing was standing; however, in Okayama some concrete structures had survived the attack. In the center of the city a six-story department store stood like a landmark (and was open for business).

The train station was also intact. As our train pulled in there were the incongruous strains of "Yankee Doodle Dandy," awkwardly played by a Japanese band. Overhead a large banner proclaimed "Welcome Victorious Occupiers!" Our advance party was on the platform, with Max Pitney grinning from ear to ear as he saluted the general. Ito, who emerged from one of the other cars, hurried over to present the governor of Okayama province and the mayor of the city. We were ushered to a vintage Cadillac, its Japanese driver standing by the open door at rigid attention. Another, younger Japanese was nearby. Ito explained that this was Tom Okamoto, who would be available to interpret for the general. Pitney laughed and said, "You'll need him—the driver does not understand a word of English." Okamoto, who could not have been five feet tall, executed a perfect Japanese bow. "I am honored, sir," he said in English with only the faintest trace of an accent, "to have been selected as your interpreter. I am a 1936 graduate of the University of Oregon."

We climbed into the car and were taken by Ito on a tour of the city. The center, except for the department store and a few other concrete structures, was all rubble; however, the eastern part of the city had escaped the fire storm. Here was a large barracks area. Our troops were already moving in. In the nearby residential area Ito took us into several houses that had been considered as possibly appropriate for the general's use as a residence. The one General Cort selected was neither the largest nor the most luxurious, but it had been the residence of the Japanese general in command of the region, and General Cort thought it suitable to his needs and appropriate to his status.

The house had two "European" rooms (i.e., rooms with hardwood floors and Western-style furniture). The rest of the house was Japanese: matted floors, sliding doors, pillows but no other furniture. General Cort had no objections to using these rooms as bedrooms, but we did bring in army mattresses and pillowcases rather than sleeping, as the Japanese did, on thin comforters with wooden headpieces. There was little we could do about the bath: It was a small wooden triangular structure in a tiny room. One could sit in the tub only with one's knees drawn closely to one's body; it was a place to get steamed but not soaked.

The Japanese had provided a household staff: a cook, a gardener, two maids, and a houseboy-interpreter. The interpreter, Harry, had been born in the United States, a Nisei whose parents had sent him (as many Japanese in the United States had done) to Japan for his college education (both for economic reasons and to avoid the widespread discrimination against Orientals in the western states). He had been in Japan at the time of the attack on Pearl Harbor and was promptly drafted into the Japanese army. But the Japanese were just as distrustful of Niseis as many people in the United States were, and so they placed them in labor battalions, mainly in locations where they were well removed from the scene of battle. Harry had been at an antiaircraft installation on an offshore island in northern Japan and, on his release from military service, had returned to Okayama where his grandparents lived. When preparations for the arrival of the occupation forces got under way, both he and his sister, Toshiko, had been virtually ordered to volunteer for assignments where their bilingual abilities could be useful. Both of them moved with us later on and were still in their respective jobs when I finally left to return to the United States in February 1947. Harry (whom I estimated to be in his mid-thirties, thus actually my senior) soon was fully accepted by the small guard detachment that had been quartered in one of the service buildings in our compound, and its sergeant asked the general's permission to have Harry move in with his group of young men.

The task of looking after the house was assigned to the second aide, Lieutenant Anderson (from Anderson, Indiana), whom General Cort had selected for this duty before our departure for Japan. He was the "house aide"; I was the "office aide." I had a desk just outside the general's office, handled all his papers, and accompanied him wherever he went. Max Pitney, in addition to commanding the artillery battalion, also served as chief of staff of the task force (the more senior commander of the Twenty-first Infantry Regiment was due to return to the United States in less than a month), and the cordial relations that Max and I had forged in the harrowing days under General Archbold developed into a genuine friendship that would last well beyond our days in Japan.[2] I liked working for Hugh Cort and came to enjoy my assignment a great deal.

General MacArthur had not yet issued his edict forbidding members of the occupation forces to accept Japanese hospitality (when he did, it was less to end fraternization than to help the Japanese conserve their scarce food supplies), and the local dignitaries felt it proper to extend invitations to the American general. Our first such outing was to the house of the prefectural governor.

Like Ito, the governor had been a member of the Japanese diplomatic corps and spoke good English. I was struck by the fact that his personal

2. In the mid-sixties Pitney, then a senior full colonel, was assigned to the University of Kansas as professor of military science. I was at the time the university's chief academic officer; thus, he reported to me. We became even better friends then and later.

library contained not only some Hemingway and T. S. Eliot but also the Nicolai and Hay ten-volume set of the Lincoln papers. But, as in any Japanese home I visited, his wife hovered on her knees in the background, waiting to serve the males who made up the party. Her *sukiyaki* was excellent, and for dessert she served French pastry that she had baked herself.

Our next invitation was quite different. The abbot of the major Buddhist monastery in the area did not speak a word of English, and neither did any of the other monks in the party. Tom Okamoto was working overtime. The menu made no concessions to our Western palates: We ate raw fish, boiled shrimp in an incredibly sharp sauce, bean curds, and other delicacies of the native cuisine.

Shortly afterward, Ito, on his daily call to find out how he could be useful to General Cort, came to me and asked if he understood correctly that I was a lawyer. When I answered in the affirmative, he told me that he had been approached by a group of local lawyers who wanted to revive the equivalent of our local bar associations and had thought that the ideal program for their first meeting would be an address by an American explaining the legal system of the United States. But since we did not have any legal officers as such with our task force, Ito had consulted the personnel officer, who had told him that, as far as he knew, there was only one legally trained American in the Okayama Task Force, and that was Lieutenant Heller.

I checked with General Cort, and he encouraged me to accept the invitation and told me to take Okamoto along to interpret for me. It was an evening meeting in a small hotel on the outskirts of the city, near the Shinto shrine where we had had dinner just two weeks earlier. There were about thirty men present, all rather elderly, all in identical black kimonos, seated on cushions along three sides of the room. I was conducted to the open side. The chairman of the meeting came forward and, with Tom Okamoto translating, expressed his pleasure that I had been able to come and his hope that the meeting would help the lawyers of the city to adapt to the new Japan. Then it was my turn to address the group.

Tom Okamoto translated my words, almost sentence by sentence. I talked about the common law tradition, the idea of the rule of law, and the place of human rights in a democracy. Given the fact that everything had to be repeated by the interpreter, there was not much time, and what I could offer was very general in nature. The audience sat in stony silence, each of the men looking straight ahead without ever moving. For someone who was accustomed to seek eye contact with his audience, it was a little disconcerting. But I forged ahead, closing at last with the kind of flourish that is standard for the typical after-dinner speech in the United States. Tom translated my conclusion, including (I presumed) my willingness to respond to questions from the audience. The silence persisted.

After a minute or two the chairman advanced, bowed deeply, and inquired whether that was the end of my remarks. I had to wonder whether he had understood what I had said but asked Tom to tell him that I had indeed concluded. The chairman bowed again and returned to his place. The silence continued. Several minutes elapsed. In a whisper, I asked Tom what was going on. "Oh," he replied, "they are honoring you. They are thinking about what you said." But shortly afterward I noticed that he was casting a nervous glance at his watch. Just then the chairman came forward again and, after the mandatory bow, addressed me. Tom turned to me with a relieved grin on his face. "Good," he said, "they liked your speech. They have invited us to stay for dinner." It occurred to me that this was a much more sensible arrangement than the American practice of feeding the speaker before one even knows whether he (or she) will say anything worthwhile.

There was another dinner that I remember, a large affair given by the governor to honor the officers of the occupation forces. Because no establishment of sufficient size and decor had survived the firebombing of the city, the dinner took place at the largest hotel in Kurashiki, a resort town about fifteen miles from Okayama near the shore of the Inland Sea. Although the governor was our host, neither he nor any other Japanese officials attended. We were asked to seat ourselves on cushions lined up on three sides of a ballroom-size, Japanese-style hall. Waitresses knelt opposite, one for every two diners, except that the general and those in his immediate party each had a waitress to himself. First, we were served Suntory whiskey; then, as the several courses were brought in, the girls began to pour sake. After a while General Cort turned to me and confided that he felt the need to do something about the considerable amount of liquid he had consumed.

I spoke to Okamoto, who was sitting on my other sidem and he said something in Japanese to the general's waitress. The girl immediately got up and, gesturing toward the doors, led the general away. When he returned, he was all smiles. "Francis," he said, "this is something you have got to experience."

I took the cue (having realized that such a trip might indeed be a good idea), and Tom alerted the girl who was my waitress. She got up, pointed toward the doors, and made a gesture inviting me to follow her. When we came to the door, she went down on her knees and pulled the door open for me. Then, after I had stepped outside, she moved, still on her knees, to the other side of the door and pulled it shut. As she got up, she again gestured me to follow her, into the garden. There, among the trees, was a small structure made of corrugated iron and painted green, so that one hardly noticed it until one was there. She gestured for me to enter. Inside I found a urinal and put it to proper use. When I came back outside, she stood there, still (or again) smiling, a pitcher in one hand from which she poured water over my hands, and a towel draped over the other arm which she offered to me to dry off. Then she pointed back toward the main building. The door-opening, door-closing routine was repeated. I returned to my place and she to hers, in front of me. Then, with evident effort, she asked in halting English: "Much better now, please?" Indeed, it had to be experienced.[3]

But these occasions in Japanese environs were the exceptions. As a rule, General Cort and I spent the evenings playing cribbage (which Anderson did not know), a bottle of Japanese whiskey between us on the table. The whiskey was part of a rather large supply our troops had found in one of the Japanese warehouses; oddly enough, it bore labels that proclaimed, in English, that its name was "Heartbrand." Hugh Cort and I thought that it was pretty good.

We were therefore taken aback when, at one of the daily staff meetings, our medical officer reported that he had sent samples of the whiskey to the Army General Hospital in Tokyo and that the laboratory there had now reported that "Heartbrand" was not fit for human consumption! He would, said the colonel, issue orders the same day to have the entire stock dumped into the river.

3. In later years "much better now, please" became an inside joke in our family.

"Not so fast, colonel," said General Cort. "What do you mean, it isn't fit? Just what would happen if I had a couple of ounces of the stuff?" The medical officer replied that, if that was the total amount consumed in the course of an evening, there might be a slight headache. "What if I had four ounces?" There would be a severe headache and possibly some blurred vision, was the answer. "Suppose that," the general pushed on, "in the course of an evening I drank a pint of the stuff?" "You would lose consciousness and there might be some brain damage," said the colonel. Hugh Cort turned to me: "If the colonel is right, Francis, then you and I have been unconscious for several weeks." The assembled officers duly chuckled; the medical officer was not amused. But General Cort put him at ease: "I don't mean to hassle you, colonel. I just happen to believe that different people react differently to liquor. You are my medical officer, and if it is your professional judgment that Heartbrand whiskey is a health hazard, then out it goes." But after the meeting he told me in private to get on the phone and call General Woodruff's aide in Kyoto (our former division commander was now chief of staff of the Sixth Army, which had its headquarters in Kyoto) and ask him to send some Suntory whiskey—in a hurry!

The Japanese, of course, found out very quickly about the dumping of the "Heartbrand" stock (we did, after all, use Japanese labor to get the job done), and "Suntory" quickly made its appearance, both on the black market and in the few clubs that had sprung up to cater to the occupation forces. Floyd Erickson, our senior pilot, persuaded the general one evening to visit what he said was the best of them, and we found it rather pleasant. It had fairly decent food, a small band played what was intended to pass for American music, and the place was spotlessly clean. When, soon afterward, General Sibert, the corps commander announced that he would come to Okayama to inspect our task force, General Cort came up with the idea that, since we had no officers' club or any other official place for relaxation or entertainment, we should take the visiting general and his party to this club.

But everything went wrong, even before we got to the club. The corps commander, his aide, and one staff officer from his G-3 (operations and training) section arrived around nine in the morning in three Piper Cubs, small two-seater planes that were normally used for artillery observation. There had been some turbulence, and the general had been airsick. He looked awful and was in a foul mood. General Cort ushered him to the Cadillac; he demanded to know why we were using a Japanese driver who, he opined, was probably just faking ignorance of English and was really a skilled agent of the Kempei-tai (the former secret police). He insisted that the car had to be driven by a member of the United States Army, and Hugh Cort told me to take the wheel. Halfway into town the car died on me.

When it comes to things mechanical, I have two left hands. I could not get the car started again. The corps commander's aide proved equally inept. So a two-star and a one-star general were bending over an ancient Cadillac's engine on an open road in Japan, trying to figure out how to bring it back to life. Fortunately, the Japanese driver was riding with two military policemen in the jeep that was following us, and he fixed the problem in short order. The corps commander told me to let the Japanese do the driving from now on.

General Cort had planned to serve the corps commander lunch at the residence. Visiting generals rather commonly prefer to take at least one meal in a troop mess, but General Cort knew that this was not our corps commander's style. He liked to have things comfortable and was known as something of a gourmand. So General Cort had told Lieutenant Anderson to set up a fancy lunch. Our Japanese cook had by this time learned (with the general as his personal instructor) to broil a steak to perfection and beyond that he could be trusted to come up with all that goes with it. We arrived at the house about ten minutes before lunch would be ready, and I served the two generals drinks in the living room. Then I left the room to check with Anderson on the lunch preparations. "Andy" assured me that he had personally checked everything. The table was set with the fine linen and the good silver we had found in the house when we moved in (and had never used before).

When time came for everyone to go to lunch Anderson opened the double doors connecting the living room and the dining room. The table did, indeed, look very good, but the centerpiece was a piece of skunk cabbage! The corps commander frowned; Hugh Cort gave me a quizzical look. Anderson did not notice anything. After lunch, our visitor retired for a short nap. Hugh Cort at once demanded to know what the big idea was to decorate the table with a weed. Anderson was evidently puzzled: He had, he said, told the gardener that we were having an important guest for lunch and that he wanted a centerpiece befitting the occasion. The gardener had told him that for such an occasion this particular plant was the proper decoration. Hugh Cort did not know whether to laugh or cry.

The evening rolled around and with it the time for our visit to the club. Hugh Cort had decided that we should have dinner at the house (but without skunk cabbage!) and visit the club afterward. We had told Erickson to alert the club manager, but to make doubly sure, while the two generals rested before dinner, I got into a jeep and drove to the club to assure myself that we would not have another skunk cabbage disaster. The manager was there and assured me that he was fully prepared for the occasion. He had even planned to have the band play ruffles, the American army's ceremonial way to salute a general officer. I told him to drop that: This was to be a private affair. He would probably lose most of his regular customers once they discovered that "the brass" was there. There was no need to overdo things.

And so we went to the club—two generals, two aides, the colonel from corps G-3, and Lieutenant Erickson. The manager was at the door, bowing repeatedly and gushing about how honored he was. We walked into the main area of the club. There, newly mounted on the balcony railing since my earlier visit, was a large sign. "For the pleasure of the occupation forces only," it read. And then it listed the prices of the various sexual pleasures the establishment was prepared to provide for its customers and the price list. The corps commander exploded; Hugh Cort got very red in the face; Floyd Erickson disappeared. As we hastily departed from the club, the manager came running after us, wringing his hands and wondering aloud what had gone wrong.

It goes without saying that Hugh Cort was relieved when the visitors left the following day. He was glad this was over, he told me, and he made it rather plain that not only did he dislike the corps commander, but he did not really care what the man might or might not say about his visit to Okayama. He was, General Cort said, one of these generals who have no concern except their own interest. His visit to Okayama was, in fact, a farewell call; the corps commander was due shortly to return to the United States and retire from the military.[4]

4. He would also, when the time came, elect to return to the United States by ship rather than by air, this in order to be able to take along a large number of crates filled with items he had "liberated" from the elegant quarters he had occupied in Kure. At his request he was met in San Francisco by three army trucks to

Throughout those fall months of 1945 the impact of the precipitous demobilization of the U.S. Army was becoming more and more noticeable. Among our officers, the large group that had opted for a ninety-day stint in Japan was leaving. Among the enlisted men, the departure rate was so high that Pvt. Jimmy Clanton, the general's nineteen-year-old orderly, wound up as first sergeant of Headquarters Battery. The replacements were few and rarely of the best kind.

Thus it was that, just as Hugh Cort was weighing whether to designate Max Pitney (an artillery officer) to command the Twenty-first Infantry Regiment or give the command to the ranking infantry officer, a major just five years out of West Point, he received a telegram advising him that a full colonel of infantry had been assigned to the Okayama Task Force and would arrive the next day. He handed me the message with the comment that "this spells trouble." When I asked him why, he pointed to the colonel's serial number: It was by more than two thousand lower than his own. I understood what that meant: On the army's permanent rank list this man was way senior to Hugh Cort, whose own rank on that list was only that of a lieutenant colonel. One could easily guess how this had come about: For probably good reasons the army had kept this man in assignments during the war where, differently from most officers of the Regular Army, he could not (and did not) qualify for temporary promotion to even a one-star general.

But General Cort was not about to display either resentment or apprehension. He told me to take the Cadillac and meet the plane on which the colonel was to arrive. He did, however, tell me to make sure that I wore all the ribbons and service awards I was entitled to. The colonel would immediately know that he was being met by a well-decorated combat veteran. I recognized the ploy.

In fact, when the colonel got out of the plane the first thing both of us did was look at the other's chest. What I saw confirmed my earlier

---

transport these boxes to his home. But also on hand were several customs agents who declared virtually everything he had brought along to be contraband and subject to customs duties. The army at first threatened him with court-martial but then allowed the matter to rest. Years afterward, when I asked Hugh Cort if he knew what had happened to the man, he said that he had disappeared—the army directory of retired officers had no entry for him. For all he knew, General Cort (himself long retired at the time) added, his former superior may have gone into the furniture business.

guess: Neither in World War I nor in this war had this man ever been in combat. His first words to me, while he was pointing at my ribbons, were: "Combat veteran, eh? When are you going home?" I told him that I had signed up to June 1947. "Are there many of you around?" he asked. "I found out after the last war that, if you have too many combat veterans around, you simply can't get the right kind of peacetime soldiering done."

I reported the conversation to General Cort who took a deep breath and observed that he understood how difficult it must be to have been a classmate of Eisenhower and Bradley and still wind up with no more rank at the end of the war than one had at the beginning. He had, he told me, talked to General Woodruff on the phone (Woodruff was also a member of that famous West Point class of 1915) and had gotten quite an earful about our new colonel. The only reassuring thing was that, so Woodruff had said, the colonel would not be with us very long: He was due to be retired just as soon as the army reverted to peacetime personnel procedures.

Hugh Cort indicated that he intended to be formal but absolutely proper in his relations with the colonel. Thus, if the general wanted the colonel to come to his office, I would go to the colonel's office, salute in the best manner, and say: "Sir, the general's compliments. The general would appreciate it if you could call on him at your early convenience." It was slightly ridiculous if it had not been so sad.

The colonel took his rank seriously. We had planned to have a parade through the center of the city on Armistice Day (as it was then still called), November 11. The general had, prior to the colonel's arrival, given the job of arranging the details of the parade to Max Pitney. By the time the colonel arrived all plans had been completed. An army band would come in from Kure, the route and the sequence of march had been established; only minor details remained to be done. Since it is customary in the army to assign the task of commander of troops for a parade to the second-in-command, General Cort asked the colonel to serve in that capacity. But our colonel demurred. The way he saw it, General Cort was the occupation commander, and he was the commander of the garrison; therefore, he should be in the reviewing stand with the general and not passing in review before him. In private General Cort uttered a few profanities, but he decided that the issue was not worth fighting over. He told me to let Max Pitney know privately what had happened and to tell him officially that he was to serve as commander of troops for the parade.

November 11 was a beautiful, sunny day. Thousands of Japanese lined the streets. The band sounded great; the troops marched in better order than I had expected. Standing behind the general, I felt tears welling up in my eyes as I saluted the colors: Yes, this was the moment of victory, even more than the day of the announcement of the surrender or the day of our arrival in Japan. I thought of "Pancho" Mendez and the others I had served with who had died along the way. But I also felt proud: This was *my* flag I was saluting, *my* country's flag, and I had done a small part to bring this day about. Hugh Cort must have felt the same way for, when the parade had ended and he had, as protocol required, thanked Max Pitney, he turned to me (and he, too, had tears in his eyes) and said, "Francis, now I believe it."

A few days later he told me that he thought he ought to pay a visit to the other two prefectures, both on the north side of the island, that were part of our zone of occupation and that it might be a good idea if I went up there and made the necessary advance arrangements. He instructed me to take a platoon of infantry with me (we had no troops of any kind in either Tottori or Shimane prefecture and this would be the first American military presence there ever). I told him that I had hoped to get to Tottori: In my days as a part-time worker in the University of Virginia library, I had run across some books by Lafcadio Hearn and had learned something about Japan, and more specifically Tottori, from that unusual author's writings.[5] Surely this was an opportunity to see Japan in its untouched state.

As the crow flies, the distance from Okayama to Tottori is less than sixty miles, but the narrow road that connected the two cities turned

5. Lafcadio Hearn, born in 1850 on a Greek island, was of Greek, English, Irish, and Japanese descent. Educated in France and England, he came to the United States in 1869 and worked as a journalist and free-lance writer, specializing in the adaptation of plots from foreign literature. He moved to Japan in 1890 where he married the daughter of a Samurai family in Tottori prefecture, became a Japanese citizen, and taught at the Imperial University of Tokyo. He adopted the lifestyle of the Japanese but continued to write in English. He died in Tottori in 1904. His works written while he lived in Japan reveal, in the words of Emily Morrison Beck, "acute understanding of character, customs, and legends of his adopted country." Louis Kronenberger, ed., *Atlantic Brief Lives* (Boston: Little, Brown and Company, 1973), 358.

and twisted as it crossed the Chikogu mountain range. Our small convoy had been on the way for nearly three hours before we crossed the divide at Kuroo Pass (2,100 feet) and the road, now barely more than a trail, began to descend. Two hours later we were met at the outskirts of the small city of Tottori by the prefectural governor and about a dozen other dignitaries. The governor insisted that I should be the guest of honor at a dinner he had planned for that evening. He sat in the back of my jeep as we rode through deserted streets to the center of the city. There, what must have been the entire population of the city was assembled, neatly divided into three groups: women on one side of the square, children on the other, men in the middle. A policeman barked a command, and everyone bowed. Then the governor gave a longish speech in Japanese which he himself repeated, sentence by sentence, in English. I responded briefly (by this time our task force had been given a small detachment of Nisei interpreters, and two of them had been assigned to my little group for this trip).

I was given what was obviously the luxury suite at the one and only hotel in town while the men were housed in the school building across the street. We had brought along an American flag, and the platoon sergeant persuaded me that we should not only hoist it from the hotel balcony, but that he should also post two sentries at the hotel's entrance. It looked rather imposing.

The governor's dinner was strictly Japanese, and most of it was fresh seafood. As we already knew from his speech, the governor spoke passable English (he had spent two years as a student at the University of London and had been a member of a trade delegation to the United States in the early thirties); the sake flowed freely, and I felt that this was a good beginning to this assignment.

But when I woke up the following morning, the town was blanketed in snow and more was coming down. The chief of police presented himself while I was eating my breakfast in the hotel dining room: The roads out of town were impassable; what were my plans? I asked him if his telephone line to Okayama was working—it was not. We tried our radio but got no reply; its limits were ten miles.

Meanwhile the snow continued to fall. There was nothing to do but sit and wait. It was obvious that we were a problem for the Japanese: There simply was nothing to eat in the little town except seafood in various forms. Even rice was scarce. At every meal the manager of the hotel would come to me with hand-wringing apologies. I assured him repeatedly, with as straight a face as I could muster, that I considered seaweed a rare treat. Some of my men were less complimentary, and at least one stole a chicken (or, rather, one was caught in the act of stealing a chicken).

At last, after three days, the snowfall came to an end. But Tottori was now buried in four feet of snow. I inquired if the town had a snowplow that might clear the westbound road to Shimane prefecture (or, alternatively, back to Okayama) for us. The answer was a predictable "so sorry." But a day later a telephone repair crew from Okayama made its way into town on foot. The road from the pass in the Chikogu range to Tottori, they said, was still impassable to vehicles, but south of the pass there had been no snow, only heavy rain. Once they had repaired the telephone line, I called Okayama and reported on our situation. We could, I suggested, leave our vehicles in Tottori and start back on foot. I estimated that it would take us six to eight hours in the heavy snow to get to the pass where we could be picked up by trucks from Okayama. Max Pitney, on the other end of the line, told me to stay put. The forecast was for warming temperatures, and, if the snow melted, we could make it back in our vehicles. My reply was that in that case we would need to have some food flown in. Pitney told me that he would check with Erickson and call me back. A half hour later he advised me that Erickson would fly over Tottori about two hours later and drop some supplies. What was needed was that I arrange for a drop area to be clearly marked.

I told the chief of police what I needed. Within an hour a large X, made of wide strips of black cloth, had been laid out on the snow in what I was told was the school's exercise area. The word, of course, got around town very quickly and, as the time approached for the plane to arrive, a large group of Japanese had gathered at the edge of the field. Most of them, so the chief of police told me, had never seen an airplane close up. About ten minutes earlier than I had expected, the L-4 became visible coming in low from the south. Erickson dropped down to about three hundred feet and flew over the field wagging his wings. On a second pass, the person riding behind him pushed out a container that landed squarely in the middle of the X. The Japanese broke into cheers. Erickson made two more passes, each time dropping another container. Then he buzzed the field and, with a last wave of his wings, headed south toward the mountains.

The three containers were amply filled. Someone had had the good sense to include a large sack of candy which I turned over to the school principal to distribute to the children. That evening I had the governor as my guest at the hotel and served him a good U.S. steak and French fries. He had brought a bottle of excellent sake. We became good friends that evening and would write to each other for a number of years. Seven years later his son was the first Japanese student to come to the University of Kansas after the war to study with me.

The following day Max Pitney told me to forget about the planned visit to Matsue, the seat of the prefectural government of Shimane, and to prepare for our return to Okayama. Erickson would fly a road reconnaissance and report on the snow conditions. In the meantime two trucks with heavy winches were starting out on the road to Tottori to provide assistance if we should need it.

We were back in Okayama two days later. General Cort never took his trip to the northern prefectures; while I was in Tottori he had been alerted about a shift of our task force to Hyogo, the prefecture directly east of Okayama, part of a realignment of occupation duties. What had been the Tenth Corps area (which, of course, included our task force) would be taken over by a composite brigade of troops from the British Commonwealth. At the same time Sixth Army was also being deactivated; all of southern Japan would come under First Corps, which our former division commander (and Hugh Cort's good friend) Roscoe Woodruff would command. A similar streamlining placed all of northern Japan under Ninth Corps (in Sendai) while overall direction of all army elements in Japan would now be with Eighth Army in Yokohama.

General Cort had also been apprised that he was to be one of many Regular Army officers whose temporary rank would be reduced and that he would move to a new assignment: Woodruff's chief of staff at First Corps. That change would be effective after he returned from a forty-five-day leave (R & R—rest and recuperation) in the States. He told me that he could arrange for me to return with him if I wanted leave at the same time; he would still be wearing his star and thus be entitled to have an aide go with him.

Then he did something very decent: He apologized for not having gotten me promoted to first lieutenant. Under wartime regulations a second lieutenant in an active combat area could be promoted to the next higher rank after just ninety days. For me this would have been on

August 15, 1945. But Hugh Cort had thought it inappropriate for him to recommend such a promotion when, in fact, on that very day the Japanese had surrendered and the war was, practically though not legally, at an end. I could not really disagree with him (and it would not have done me any good, anyhow). He assured me that he would send my papers of promotion to the division commander (who was authorized to approve promotions at this level) on November 15. But two weeks before that date the War Department decreed that it would now take eighteen months at a minimum for a second lieutenant to be advanced in rank, and the recommendation had to go through channels all the way to the theater commander (i.e., General MacArthur). So I was still a "shavetail" and would retain that rank until late November 1946.

To Hugh Cort's great pleasure I had made application for a commission in the Regular Army. I had thought about this for quite a while and had finally decided that I might actually make a fairly good officer. Of course, I could go back to graduate school, finish my doctorate and hope for a teaching job. But I was not so sure that this was really what I wanted to do. With Father Louis dead and Eleanor married to another no strong ties drew me back to Charlottesville. More important, I had met some truly fine people in the army: General Lester, Livy Taylor, "Tommy" Lang, Max Pitney, and Hugh Cort, to say nothing of the men I had shared the days of combat with: "Black Jack" Harris, Austin Flack, Carmel Wallace, "Targo," and all the rest. Yes, there had been General Archbold, but I counted him an exception to the rule and, anyhow, in the end the army had taken care of him.

If I intended to remain in the service it would be important for me to get assignments that would be useful to my future career. I talked this over with General Cort. He told me that he could probably arrange to have me transferred to First Corps (where he would be) if I wanted, but, of course, as a colonel he was no longer entitled to an aide, and on a corps staff there was little need for junior officers. What I should do, once my R & R was over, was return to the Twenty-fourth Division where my assigned duties would, of course, be up to the new people in charge. He told me something else: There is a certain risk involved in spending too much time as a general's aide; one can get labeled as "So-and-so's boy." This, of course, was the reason for the regulation that provided that anyone who had served six months or more as an aide could, without prejudice, decline another similar assignment. That did not mean much to me at the time, but three months later I would be offered just such duty (by General Lester) and, remembering Hugh Cort's advice, would decline it.

Meanwhile the general went about directing the preparations for the move to the prefectural seat of Hyogo, at Himeji. While I was taking notes as we went along, he inspected possible sites for troop housing, location of the division headquarters, training areas, etc. Himeji had suffered relatively little damage. Its imposing castle, truly a picture-postcard sight, was virtually unharmed, but it was also virtually uninhabitable. Differing from Okayama, the Japanese had not had any major troop units in Himeji. This made it necessary to disperse our troops, and now it almost seemed a blessing that our troop strength had shrunk so drastically. By this time, wherever there were supposed to be three of something, there were only two: two infantry battalions, each of two companies, each of only two platoons, and each platoon with only two squads. In Max Pitney's artillery battalion half the howitzers had been put in storage; there simply were not enough men around to keep twelve guns clean and operable.

At the same time the general and I began to make our preparations for the trip home. He dug out his good uniform and had it sent to Kyoto where the army had set up a laundry and dry-cleaning plant. I was able to buy a set of "pinks and greens" from a recently arrived officer who (for whatever reasons) had come with two sets. General Woodruff's aide got me a pair of (normal) shoes, proper socks, and a couple of shirts from the only army store in Japan that stocked such items (in Tokyo, of course) as well as a "val-pack" for my belongings.

Traveling with a general has its advantages. On the train to Tokyo we had a compartment to ourselves as far as Osaka where we were joined by another general and his aide who were also headed for Tokyo. When we arrived in that city, an army staff car took us to Atsugi airfield where we were ushered into a private waiting area and served dinner. Both in Guam and in Honolulu we were taken to the base commander's residence and accorded generous hospitality (most important and welcome, the use of a shower). We were flying in a C-47 which, in addition to Guam and Honolulu, also made stops on Kwajalein and Johnson Islands.

When we approached San Francisco, the pilot did a full circle over the bay and welcomed us back to the U.S.A. There were cheers from everyone on the plane. Whoever had been gone the longest, the pilot announced, was entitled to free drinks that day at the men's bar of the Mark Hopkins Hotel. With my more than three years I easily won that contest.

Our landing at Hamilton Field meant parting from Hugh Cort. He gave me a bear-hug and told me that I would always be his second son. Then he was taken to a lounge for distinguished visitors to await a plane that would take him to San Antonio and a reunion with his family. I had a big lump in my throat. Even though we had known each other for less than a year, my early respect for him had grown into genuine affection. He was not only a fine officer but one of the most genuinely decent human beings I had ever met. I owed him then (and still do) a great deal.

I boarded a bus into San Francisco, put my bag into a locker at the bus station, exchanged my aide's insignia for the field artillery's crossed cannons, and headed for the Mark Hopkins, just a few blocks away. I had not been in the hotel bar for more than twenty minutes when who should walk in but my brother Tom. It was not an accident: A week earlier in the same bar he had noticed and then introduced himself to a lieutenant colonel with field artillery insignia and a Twenty-fourth Division shoulder patch. It turned out to be Max Pitney who had told him that I was due in San Francisco just a few days later. Tom had checked the bar every afternoon since that day.

He had been discharged from the army in September 1945, had joined his wife in San Francisco, and was now attending the University of California in Berkeley. I spent three or four days with Tom and Catherine at their apartment in Richmond. Tom was full of great plans; when I told him that I was considering staying in the service, he told me I was crazy. (But three years later—by then an honor graduate of the ROTC, and divorced—he accepted a commission in the Regular Army and spent nearly thirty years on active service.)

I took a train to the East Coast. Only then did I realize what the war may have meant to the people back home. When I went to the dining car on the first evening I was given a seat across from an elderly couple. After some small talk the man asked me if he was right, that the first of the ribbons I wore was that of the Silver Star Medal. When I told him that it was, he stood up, tapped his glass for silence, and then announced to all persons in the dining car that they had a hero in their midst, and would they all drink to all the American heroes of the war. I had never thought of myself as a hero and was genuinely embarrassed. But I also recognized that this was as close as many of these people had come to someone who had been in the midst of combat action. After that first meal there was hardly another meal aboard the train at which someone did not invite me to eat as their guest.

I had called my parents from San Francisco and again from Chicago, so they were prepared for my arrival. They were living in a small apartment on East Fifty-ninth Street; *grandmère* (my stepmother's French mother) was staying with them, and after a few days I found the situation rather confining. After about ten days in New York, during which I drank far more than I needed, I traveled to Charlottesville and spent another week there. But in neither place was there much for me to do. I visited with friends and acquaintances, but, on the whole, I soon began to look forward to going back to Japan and, perhaps more important, a job to be done.

Thus, I was rather pleased when, on my arrival at Hamilton Field, a colonel I had met through Hugh Cort offered to let me take his place on a plane going out the same evening. The medical officer looked at me in surprise when I asked him to give me all four of the required shots at once; as a rule he administered one shot a day, an arrangement that allowed those traveling to the Far East to spend four more days in San Francisco without having them count against their leave entitlement.

My seatmate on the plane was a civilian, a political science professor from Northwestern University whose name (Kenneth Colegrove) I recognized as that of one of the few reputable American specialists on Japanese government. He was on his way to Tokyo to serve as a consultant at MacArthur's headquarters on the implementation of the new Japanese constitution. I talked more political science and law in the next ten hours than I had even thought about in four years.

I had no difficulty getting a seat on the army train to Himeji and, on my arrival there, asked the military police detachment for transportation to the task force headquarters. The young driver barely found his way there and generally seemed to know very little. I asked him who the new general was, and he could not tell me. When I arrived at headquarters, the adjutant, another face I had never seen before, did not give me the opportunity to ask: Almost as soon as we had shaken hands (and he had mumbled his name) he told me that the general had already been notified of my arrival and was expecting me.

I walked into the general's office to report and instantly recognized the man who returned my salute: It was the general I had ordered to help with the digging on the beach at Leyte! The desk plate read "Brigadier General C. C. Blanchard." As he told me to have a seat he said that he was sure that we had met before, but he could not remember where or under what circumstances. With some trepidation I reminded him of our A-Day encounter on Leyte; surely, I said to myself, this was a ticket straight to the crummiest job in the entire division artillery. But he surprised me: Yes, he remembered the occasion, he said, and he thought now as he had thought then (and indeed had told me) that I had acted correctly. He glanced at my record, which was on his desk, and observed that I had signed up to stay until June 1947: There was a vacancy at the moment in the position of assistant S-2 (i.e., survey officer) at the headquarters that would be my assignment. But he also told me that the captain who was in the S-2 (intelligence) slot was due for rotation back to the States in another thirty days and then I would succeed to his job—a major's slot for a second lieutenant: General Blanchard had more confidence in me than I had any reason to expect. I assured him that I would do my level best. Thus began nearly a year of service on "Charley" Blanchard's staff. It would take me to another of Japan's main islands: Kyushu.

Fukuoka, Japan

On a map, Kyushu, the southernmost of the Japanese main islands, bears some resemblance to the African continent. At its northernmost point it faces the western tip of the main island of Honshu, across a strait narrow enough that a railroad tunnel connected the two islands (and a second tunnel, for automobile traffic, was later added). At the top of Kyushu lies Kokura, the "Pittsburgh of Japan,"[1] already selected as our division headquarters. Fukuoka, the capital of the prefecture of the same name, is about eighteen miles southwest of Kokura, on a large bay protected by a narrow peninsula, Hakata. Further south on the west coast, below Fukuoka prefecture, are the cities of Sasebo and Nagasaki, the latter, of course, the target of the second atomic bomb. On the east side of the island there are few cities and none toward the southern tip until one reaches Kagoshima. The original plan for the American invasion of the Japanese home islands had called for the initial landings to be made at and near Kagoshima.

When the American forces first occupied Japan, the responsibility for Kyushu was assigned to the Thirty-third Infantry and the Sixth Marine divisions. By the spring of 1946, both divisions had been deactivated

1. In recent years, Kokura has been absorbed into the highly industrialized metropolis of Kita-Kyushu.

or returned to the United States and the Twenty-fourth Infantry Division assigned to take their place.[2] General Blanchard had already visited our new area (Fukuoka prefecture) and had decided that the troops would be housed on a former Japanese air base on the Hakata Peninsula where, eventually, facilities for all personnel (including housing for dependents) would be erected. Until that time, Divarty headquarters would be in the city of Fukuoka.

We of Divarty set up in the locations previously used by the marines. Thus officers stationed in the city (as opposed to those on Hakata) occupied the top two floors of a five-story hotel, the Shinko-tei. The dining room and rooms for social activities (pool, cards, etc.) were on the top floor; our living quarters were on the floor below. The hotel had been designed to accommodate persons arriving by rail from Honshu and having business in the downtown area of the city; the lower floors were still used for that purpose. The building had not been harmed during the war, and all rooms were comfortable and well furnished Western-style. The kitchen staff produced excellent meals; the bar was usually well stocked, and its prices were low: we lived well.

The main drawback was that we were quite far from our headquarters, miles away from the motor pool, and even farther away from the four battalions. Most of us took to pedestrian ways to get from the hotel to our headquarters building, but the fairly regular rains made that a less-than-satisfactory solution. Back east in Yokohama, where Eighth Army headquarters was located, there was concern also about security (and appearances); thus, we soon started to look for a facility that would provide more privacy and better security.

A few weeks later we moved from the Shinko-tei to a smaller hotel that had the advantage of being self-contained and included an enclosed area where our jeeps could be parked. The cooks and maids went along with us, and the good life continued. We had brought a few Japanese with us, including Harry, the young interpreter from the general's residence in Okayama, and his sister, Toshiko. Oka, a somewhat austere

2. The areas previously assigned to the Forty-first Division (the western part of Honshu) and to the Twenty-fourth (the island of Shikoku) and the prefectures on Honshu that had been assigned to "Task Force Cort," became the responsibility of a brigade of troops from the British Commonwealth.

young man, who had become part of our camp following during the time in Himeji, also moved with us to Kyushu.

Oka was an interesting person. The son of an American newspaper correspondent and a Japanese mother, he was tall and lanky, with his father's blue eyes but typically Japanese straight black hair. Although he had never been outside Japan, he spoke flawless English. Like Harry, he had spent the war in a unit of the Japanese army on one of the smaller islands. The most remarkable thing about Oka was his broad knowledge and understanding of English and American literature. He read voraciously and could wax enthusiastic if someone handed him a volume by Thomas Hardy or a story by Hemingway. In addition, he was a capable bookkeeper and thus was the ideal choice to be the storekeeper for our small hotel. (In later years, he would be a highly successful businessman in Tokyo.)

Brig. Gen. Charles C. Blanchard, called "Tizzy" behind his back, was an easy man to work for. He had an even temper, and he knew what was expected of him. More important, he knew how to use his staff. He told us what to do and expected us to do it right. That was not quite the way the new executive officer, Col. Paul Walters, operated. A West Pointer like Blanchard, Walters was probably smarter than the general, but he was often tense and nervous and did not always give the rest of us enough time or slack to get our assignments done before he would come around to check on progress. But he had a certain amount of style, and outside of duty hours he was great company. I soon came to respect and like him. When we met again, thirty years later, we were still congenial.

The S-3 (operations and training) was also new and also a product of West Point, but there the similarity with our two superiors ended. Maj. Ulysses S. Grant Jones (his real name) and I never did hit it off. Quite the opposite was the case in my relationship with the fourth West Pointer on the staff, Maj. William W. Cover. "Willie," who was so short that he had needed a waiver to get into the military academy, was a delightful person. Well read, with a fine sense of humor, he was my kind of person. We soon became fast friends, and we continued our relationship until his death in 1993.

My own duties as S-2 (intelligence) of the headquarters were many and varied. The Japanese were still under orders from MacArthur to gather and surrender all military supplies. In anticipation of an American invasion, most supplies had been widely dispersed throughout the country. The marines had pretty well taken care of the caches of weapons and ammunition, but items such as uniforms, blankets, fuel, and food reserves were still being located and collected. The process was still going on; part of my job was to organize patrols that crisscrossed the prefecture and, with the help of the local police, looked for these stores.

It occurred to me more than once that, had the situation been reversed, if the Japanese had prevailed and were occupying the United States, these stores would have disappeared even before the first occupation forces had landed. But at least in the rural areas I came to know, it would not have occurred to the population to touch what had been placed in their midst by their government. Thus it was relatively easy to locate the hidden supplies. Once they had been found and inventoried, it was my job (within guidelines from MacArthur's headquarters) to determine what was to be confiscated and destroyed and what was to be turned over to the Japanese for distribution to the needy, of whom, of course, there were tens of thousands. The actual work of gathering and dispersing the supplies was left to the Japanese police, who were every bit as conscientious about this task as the populace had been in leaving the supplies intact.

Fukuoka was a main port for repatriation of Koreans being returned from Japan to Pusan, in a homeland many of them had never seen,[3] and of Japanese being returned from China and Manchuria through the port city of Huladao, north of Peking (now called Beijing). Again the Japanese handled all the actual work but the overall supervision of the operation was my responsibility. The procedures included screening and searching the Koreans, who used every conceivable ruse to take valuables out of Japan. SCAP (or Supreme Commander Allied Powers) had instructed the Japanese government that the Koreans were not to be allowed to take gold or silver out of the country, but there was hardly a day that the search operations did not yield everything from gold bullion to minute grains of silver. As time went by, we collected so much of the precious metals that I needed four men to assist me when, after six months, on instructions from SCAP, I took the accumulated treasure to the imperial mint in Osaka.

3. Korea had been treated as occupied territory since 1910.

As far as the returning Japanese were concerned, our main interest was information that might be of military value, especially about Manchuria, which had been occupied by the Soviet Union for more than a decade. For this purpose I had a twenty-man detachment of Nisei interrogators, headed by a Lieutenant Hideki, a Nisei who had graduated from the University of Wisconsin. The job of this team was to interrogate all officers and senior NCOs, as well as those civilians who, by virtue of their occupation or education, could be assumed to be observant. Once a week I extracted what seemed to me important from the interrogation reports prepared by the team and sent it directly to the G-2 at First Corps in Kyoto. He, in turn, consolidated my reports with those from the other two repatriation centers (at Nagoya and Nagasaki) and forwarded this report to the G-2 at Eighth Army headquarters in Yokohama; from there they were sent to MacArthur's headquarters in Tokyo. Before long, I was quite familiar with place names like Bikin, Khabarovsk, and Ussuriysk.

The actual interrogation I left entirely to the Nisei detachment, but I had given a standing instruction that I was to be called whenever an officer of higher rank was to be questioned. This was in accordance with my orders from corps that anyone with vital information was to be sent on promptly to Kyoto for interrogation. But this never happened: colonels and generals simply did not appear among those being repatriated to Japan from the Russian-held areas.

When I took charge of this operation, it was not clear who was in charge at the other end of the pipeline in Huladao. In Pusan, where the returning Koreans were debarked, we knew that we were dealing with American occupation personnel; one could talk to them easily by telephone, and it was possible (as I did early on) to fly across for consultations and visits.

The situation was quite different with respect to China. The marine colonel who preceded me had left me a memorandum deploring the fact that he had been unable to establish any kind of direct communication with Huladao. He thought that the earlier transports had been dispatched by troops of the (Communist) Eighth Route Army but that more recently the Huladao operation was being handled by government (i.e., Chiang Kai-shek's) forces. In any case, the colonel's memorandum continued, there was no contact with the mainland embarkation point (and the Japanese harbormaster confirmed that information).

I decided to try a direct approach and, with Lt. Hideki's assistance, spoke to the captain of one of the two Japanese ships that brought the returnees from China to Japan. I gave him two bottles of bourbon, one for himself and one, with my compliments, for the Chinese colonel I understood to be in charge in Huladao, and asked him to find out whether the Chinese would be willing to have me come over for a brief visit. Two weeks later he was back with a small gift for me from Colonel T'eng and a formal invitation to come. Along with the invitation was the name of a Chinese liaison officer in Tokyo who was in radio contact with Huladao. Luckily the man spoke passable English. He had already been notified of my intended visit and gave me some dates that seemed suitable.

Now I thought that I should really get approval from my higher-ups. The colonel at First Corps thought it was an excellent idea, but the general at Eighth Army wanted to switch the invitation to himself. I called Hugh Cort, now the chief of staff of the corps, and he got the corps commander, his old friend General Woodruff, to vouch for me. My trip was promptly approved.

The passage was uneventful. I was met at Huladao by a Chinese captain who spoke fair English and who escorted me to a guesthouse. I would meet Colonel T'eng, he said, at a dinner that the colonel was holding in my honor that evening. I had, at General Blanchard's suggestion, brought along the "pinks and greens" I had bought before my leave as well as a small bottle of salad oil. As a lieutenant, Blanchard had served a tour of duty in China where he had learned what he called the salad trick: line your stomach by drinking some salad oil before you sit down to be sociable with Orientals. I had also put on all my ribbons. When the captain came for me at 8:00 P.M., I was ready.

Colonel T'eng did not speak a word of English but seemed delighted to have an opportunity to throw a party. There were about a dozen Chinese officers in attendance, and the banquet lasted more than four hours. It included all the celebrated elements of traditional Chinese feasting: swallow's nest soup, fried dog, etc., and an almost unending line of toasts with hellishly strong Chinese liquor. It was a good thing that I had followed General Blanchard's recommendation of the salad trick.

On the following day I was given a full tour of the base, including a detailed review of the processing procedures. I discovered why there was so much evident fear among the repatriates arriving in Fukuoka:

The Chinese were telling them that the Americans would detain anyone whom they, the Chinese, reported as not fully cooperative with them.

On the third day, the captain took me, in an American jeep, on a tour of the countryside. It was hilly and altogether attractive, although the villages we passed through seemed to be no more than agglomerations of miserable hovels. I left feeling that I had accomplished my purpose, that I now had some understanding of the conditions at the other end of the line. A few weeks later, at my invitation, the captain came over to Fukuoka for a return visit. I could not persuade Colonel T'eng to come.

Repatriation was not my only duty outside the responsibilities normally assigned to an artillery intelligence officer. Shortly after we arrived in Fukuoka, the small U.S. Navy detachment that had supervised port operations was withdrawn, and it became one of my duties to keep up with harbor traffic and port operations. Technically, I was the United States Navy port director and in that capacity reported to a rear admiral sitting in Yokohama. (I never saw him and do not recall his name.) My duties as port director were minimal. Once a day the Japanese harbormaster talked to my interpreter to report that there was nothing unusual to report, and he also sent over a list of the previous day's arrivals and departures and a traffic forecast for the next several days. Most of the time there were only small trading ships, usually of Japanese registry, though occasionally there were also Chinese vessels, and once or twice a month a Dutchman based in the East Indies would put in.

Thus there was considerable excitement when word came that a British Indian destroyer was expected and would wish to stay in port for several days. As we had anticipated, while the crew was Indian, the officers were British. We invited them ashore and had some of the nurses and Red Cross girls from the local army hospital join us. (Eventually the destroyer's executive officer married "Tex," the best-looking of the Red Cross girls.) The Britishers were eager for American beer, and we were willing to swap beer for Scotch (of which they had plenty on board).

Toward the end of their stay they invited some of us to dinner aboard the ship. There was roast beef and lots of whiskey straight and, of course, without ice. Mercifully, when we came ashore, a U.S. Army truck was there, as none of us were fit to drive. I found out afterward that the Japanese chief of police had received a report from one of his men who was patrolling the dock area that there was a very loud party aboard the destroyer and that one of the jeeps parked on the pier belonged to Lieutenant Heller. (The chief was looking out for us.) He decided to call our quarters and, with Oka's help, got one of the officers there to arrange for the truck to come and pick us up.

Intelligence operations required that I stay in touch with other U.S. intelligence units in the area. This included the A-2 of the army air base at Itazuke, not far south of Fukuoka, and in the city itself a large censorship detachment, a criminal investigation detachment (CID), and a counterintelligence (CIC) unit. There were weekly meetings of the officers in charge of these several intelligence activities in addition to frequent contacts by telephone or through personal visits.

In practice, however, my most important and most frequent contact was the Japanese chief of police of the prefecture. I had a phone on my desk that connected me directly with this official (whose name I regrettably do not recall), and there was rarely a day that we did not use the direct line. Fortunately, the chief spoke fairly good English, but I also made frequent use of the interpreter I had inherited from the marine corps colonel who had previously handled most of the tasks that were now mine.

The interpreter, Shidei Matsuoka, was a man in his fifties who had served for over twenty years as administrative assistant and translator for the (British) manager of the Shell Oil Company refinery on the Hakata peninsula. He showed me once where his spacious and comfortable home had been before it had been destroyed in a firebombing by our air force. Now Matsuoka and his family of four lived in a one-room shack on the outskirts of the city. He told me that, during much of the war, after his boss had been interned as an enemy alien, he (Matsuoka) had been paid by the Japanese government to act as caretaker for the plant which, since the Japanese could not bring in any crude oil, was standing idle. Toward the end, however, he had been drafted and in the final months of the war was digging gun emplacements on the slopes of Mount Fuji in anticipation of the American invasion of the Japanese home islands.

My predecessor had left me a letter urging me to keep Matsuoka, whom he had found helpful and reliable. A year later I made the same recommendation to my successor. But I discovered within the first two weeks that Matsuoka found me somewhat different from the colonel for whom he had previously worked.

Matsuoka had brought me an invitation to dinner from the chief of police. By that time MacArthur's decree forbidding American occupation personnel to accept invitations to meals from Japanese was already in effect; Matsuoka knew that, as did the chief. But Matsuoka impressed on me that it was most important that not only the chief but also the senior officers should get to know me and there was no better way to do this than over food and drinks. I checked with General Blanchard, and he told me to go ahead. This was my introduction to the "salad trick": Since I would be alone and there would be a group (I did not know how many) of the Japanese, with each of whom I would have to exchange a toast, General Blanchard told me to drink a few spoonfuls of salad oil before going to the party to lessen the impact the alcohol might have on me. I followed the general's advice then as well as before Colonel T'eng's party in Huladao.

To Matsuoka's consternation I walked to the small restaurant where the party was to take place (the marine colonel had used a staff car, but we had no such luxuries; it would be several months before General Blanchard was able to exchange the rickety Cadillac General Cort had acquired in Okayama for a standard army vehicle of the type authorized for general officers).

There were twelve Japanese police officers present, all in their Sunday-best Western dark suits. Poor Matsuoka looked rather run-down by comparison. We settled down on a square of cushions and were served Suntory whiskey. Then came appetizers, mostly raw fish, some of it in marinades, and the standard bean-curd soup. There was more whiskey. The main course was an excellent *sukiyaki*, accompanied by an equally good sake. The chief proposed a toast. I had already learned that, while I would not be expected to offer a toast in return, it would be grossly impolite if I did not empty my glass. This, of course, was the point of General Blanchard's warning, for now each of the Japanese in turn toasted me. And each of them came around with his glass of whiskey, and with each of them I had to empty my glass. Because Matsuoka was of "my" party, the toastmakers also drank with him; shortly afterward he curled up in a corner and went to sleep. I could tell that I had been drinking a good deal, but, thanks to the oil coating of my stomach, I felt very little effect.

The Japanese were obviously impressed by my capacity. But they were also quite prepared for the contrary. They showed me a small room behind our banquet area where, to my astonishment, there was a U.S. Army hospital bed, made up with clean sheets and covered with blankets from the same source. This, I was told, had been put here by the marine colonel who, after the initial party for him, had frequently returned to the restaurant and enjoyed the company of the resident geishas. I was most welcome, I was assured, to avail myself of these conveniences. They were somewhat appalled when I not only declined but insisted that I would return to the hotel on foot and by myself. Matsuoka did not appear for work the next day, but when he showed up the following day, he told me that the chief of police had told him that my Japanese hosts were most impressed with my performance that evening. It was quite obvious that Matsuoka was no less impressed.

I soon discovered that it did not hurt to have the chief on my side because in many ways I depended on him. Not only did I need his full cooperation to fulfill the tasks assigned to me, but quite often his channels of communication worked better than mine, and he was able to apprise me of directives coming down from Tokyo that he had received directly while my information had to come through channels: from SCAP in Tokyo to Eighth Army in Yokohama to First Corps in Kyoto to the Twenty-fourth Division in Kokura to me in Fukuoka.

On one occasion that I recall, for instance, the chief called me to get my instructions about the arrival of a party of Thai citizens,[4] including the embassy's chargé d'affaires and his family. They were due the next day, and, said the chief, our headquarters was to see to it that they were properly quartered and put aboard the ship that was to return them to Bangkok. The ship, so the Japanese harbormaster advised me a few minutes later, was due to dock within the hour. The information about all of this did not reach me through our own channels until days after the Thais had sailed for home!

The chief suggested that there was a Japanese hotel that might be able to accommodate the hundred-plus Thais though he doubted that the manager had enough food on hand to feed so large a group. He and I went to look at the hotel and discussed arrangements with the manager. He showed us where and how he might be able to house the

4. Then still called Siamese.

visitors but said that he had provisions for only about a dozen people. I told the chief of police to check the warehouses where the confiscated military stocks were kept; he was able to find enough food to solve the major part of the problem. I got our supply officer to turn over a small amount of meat and some bread and milk. On a return visit that evening the manager showed me the rooms he was having prepared for the chargé and his family and the two or three other diplomats of lesser rank who, so the chief's information indicated, were also in the party. The chief arranged for several trucks to take most of the visitors from the railhead to the hotel and then, the next day, to the ship. For the diplomats, he located a couple of old limousines to take them in something resembling style.

The arrival of the group went smoothly. The chargé d'affaires and his wife both spoke passable English and seemed grateful for the attention given to their needs. I did not accompany them to the hotel but told them that I would come by later in the day to assure myself that everything was in order. But I was in for a surprise. Each entrance to the hotel was now festooned with a large and conspicuous sign that announced "Off Limits! Venereal Disease. By Order of the Provost Marshal." I had neglected to tell Lt. Al Roth, the provost marshal, that I was going to use the hotel and for what purpose. Fortunately the chargé d'affaires took the incident with good humor.

Another episode that was somewhat embarrassing to me occurred when one of my patrols called in, quite excitedly, from Kurume, a mining city about twenty-five miles south of Fukuoka (and the site, during the war, of one of the more notorious prisoner-of-war camps). The sergeant reported that he had run into a ring of persons that was selling girls into servitude. He had placed four men under arrest and taken them to the local police station.

Even as we talked, the phone connected to that of the chief of police rang. He had heard of the arrest and wanted to know what the charges were. I stalled him, and my sergeant and I got on the phone to the division G-2 in Kokura, who told me to check with First Corps in Kyoto. The colonel there asked me, with unmistakable sarcasm, if I had read my SCAP directives. If I had, I would know that MacArthur had not told the Japanese to suppress such transactions, only that Japanese courts were not to enforce the contracts. The mere fact that a farmer would sell his daughter was not forbidden. There was no charge that could be levied against either the seller or the buyer. The four men should be released at once.

I informed the chief of police and gave appropriate instructions to the sergeant in Kurume. The sergeant followed my orders and returned the four men, with apologies, to their homes. But rather than return their business ledgers to them he brought the large, leather-bound, gold-cut volumes to me. I had no right to do so, but I carried these books back to the States with me where eventually they came to repose in the library of the University of Virginia where they may still be.

In addition to sending out patrols throughout the week, I soon made it a practice to make Sunday excursions into areas of the prefecture that the patrols had not yet visited. By this time I had acquired a fair amount of everyday Japanese, enough to be able to ask for directions and make small talk. I soon learned that, as my jeep moved through remote villages, word of my coming would precede me. (The chief had informed all stations in the prefecture that the American officer in a jeep marked VJ-2 was to be treated with due respect; I suspect a report on his visit was to be phoned in to the chief's office at once.) Thus, as I came to the next settlement, the local police officer would be alerted and, quite frequently, be awaiting my arrival, often accompanied by some of the village elders.

I recall an occasion when one such reception committee insisted that I should call on their old doctor who, they said, had studied in America. To be sure, there in the old man's office hung a diploma from the medical school of the University of Pennsylvania, dated 1905! He had never been back nor did he remember much of the English language. But it was obvious that he was pleased by the attention garnered by my visit to his home.

On another Sunday it rained so hard that I decided to forego my planned trip to a distant village. Instead I decided to visit the Imperial University, on the northern outskirts of the city. I asked to see the librarian and was shortly ushered into the study of an old gentlemen who told me that after a lifetime of teaching history he had been put in charge of the library. As behooved a visitor, I did not ask any questions until we had finished drinking tea. Then I assured my host that I had no intention of removing anything from his library but that I had a personal interest in books and libraries and just wanted to see what he had. For instance, I asked, what kind of books did he have available if someone wanted to learn about the United States and its government? He explained that the reader would have to leave a request and then his staff would search the catalog to identify and locate the books. (I recalled that this had also been the procedure at the library of the University of Vienna and probably most European libraries in those days.)

I asked him how the catalog was organized, and he produced an oversize volume bound in dull white leather: It was actually not a catalog at all but merely an acquisitions record. I proceeded to explain to him how American libraries were set up and, in response to his question, wrote down the major categories of the Library of Congress cataloging system (which I had learned while working as a student assistant at the University of Virginia library before I had been drafted).

My host escorted me to the university's main gate and invited me to return soon. About six months later Matsuoka reported that the old gentleman had called to say he would be honored if I would have a cup of tea with him at my convenience. I told Matsuoka to accept the invitation for the following Sunday. That Sunday, after the tea routine was over, my host told me that he had something he wanted to show me. He escorted me into the stacks and proudly pointed to the books: The spines bore a combination of Western-style letters and numbers, "A 1," "A 2," etc. The collection looked just like a standard American library except that the books were still shelved in the order in which they had been acquired; not a book had been moved. There was absolutely no correlation between the numbers on the spines and the content of the books nor was there a card catalog. I did not criticize the arrangement. He had done the best he could based on his understanding of the American method.

Far and away the most exciting happening during my stay in Fukuoka, however, was the visit of a Russian submarine in the Tsushima islands. The Tsushimas, known to history buffs as the site of the decisive naval battle of the Russo-Japanese war of 1895–1896, are roughly halfway between Kyushu and Korea. The marines had originally placed a platoon of infantry there but, as demobilization set in, had been forced to withdraw it. We simply took over the arrangements they had then made: The Japanese chief of police in the islands' principal town, Izuhara, had been given an American radio and instructions to check in at certain times or whenever anything unusual occurred.

For several months the report was always the same: "Nothing to report." Then one day, the Tsushima radio crackled at an unscheduled time. I got Matsuoka to the radio, and at once he got terribly excited: The Russians had landed! A Soviet submarine had put in at Izuhara, allegedly because it was in need of repairs, and the captain did not want to wait on the high seas for the arrival of the repair ship. I checked with my Japanese police chief, and he confirmed that he had just received the same report and had passed it on to Tokyo. I called Kyoto where my information caused considerable agitation. We should, said the colonel, find out the facts for ourselves.

I checked with the Japanese harbormaster to see if there was a boat that could take me there. The sea, he said, was too rough for small craft, and there was no larger vessel available. I asked Lt. Erickson if he could fly me over, but he said that the weather was too rough for a light plane to attempt the trip over water. So I called my counterpart at Itazuke air base.

He thought there was no problem getting a plane over the Tsushimas, but, of course, there was no landing area for anything but the smallest planes. I told him that, as a result of my Alamo Scouts training, I was a qualified parachutist, but he called my attention to the fact that Itazuke only had fighter planes, not the kind of craft normally used for parachute jumps. I told him that should make no difference.

In the meantime the phone had begun to ring from Kyoto. The information had now reached Tokyo, and General Willoughby, MacArthur's intelligence chief, wanted an immediate reconnaissance made. I told the colonel that I had already made my plans and would be leaving within the hour. I called my air corps friend again and told him I was ready to go. He said he would have to get clearance from his colonel. It occurred to me that I had better tell General Blanchard what I intended to do. I stressed that my order had come through intelligence channels from Tokyo; that got me the general's approval (my air corps co-conspirator used the same approach, with equal success).

Of course, my air corps friend had insisted that he would pilot the plane I used. An hour later we were in the air in an A-26 fighter-bomber. When we got over Tsushima, I climbed over the side of the plane onto the wing, and from there I jumped. The air was exceedingly rough, and I began to doubt my ability to maneuver to my intended landing point. I knew that there was a large playing field near the high school at the north edge of Izuhara, and I had, through Matsuoka, told the local chief of police that this was where I would come in. Luckily, with considerable tugging and pulling of the parachute's strings, I was in fact able to land there.

The local chief had had enough sense (or perhaps Matsuoka had suggested it to him) to have the high school's English teacher there to interpret for me. The Russians, I was told, were wandering all over town as if they owned it, insisting that merchants accept rubles in return for purchases. And they had the women of the town thoroughly scared because of an incident shortly after their landing which only the intervention of the sub's commander had kept from ending in physical violence.

The commander, I was told, mostly stayed aboard the submarine, but he had spent a little time in town, taking some of his meals at the one and only inn. This was where I met him shortly afterward. He was a fairly young man, perhaps two or three years older than I. His knowledge of English equaled my knowledge of Russian, but eventually we discovered that we could communicate in French. I asked him why he had not cleared his intentions to put into port with our occupation authorities, and he told me that his engine problems had come up quite suddenly. Had he asked his superiors about checking with us? His answer was vague; in fact, reading between his words, I became convinced that he was acting on orders and that his mission was to find out what reaction there would be to a showing of the Soviet flag in these islands. It became clear to me that he was extremely cautious not to be drawn into any conversation that might give me more information. Later on in the day, when the weather cleared, he and I sat on the pier and had a long conversation about Russian and French literature. He had no difficulty understanding me, but if I asked about anything that pertained to the sub, its condition, or the intended length of its stay, he seemingly lost the ability to understand even the simplest words in the French language.

The next morning a Russian submarine tender appeared and dropped anchor offshore. A small boat brought in what purported to be a repair crew. Whatever ailed the sub was fixed within half an hour. Then, without a word of good-bye from either crew, both tender and sub departed.

The winds had calmed almost completely, and Erickson was able to pick me up for the return flight to Fukuoka. As soon as I was back at my desk, I called the colonel in Kyoto. An hour later he called back:

General Willoughby wanted me to report to him in person and as soon as possible.

I took the night train to Tokyo and at the appointed hour presented myself at the office of the assistant chief of staff, G-2, at SCAP headquarters in the Dai-Ichi building. Maj. Gen. Charles Willoughby, a native German who had risen through the ranks from private to two-star general, was an impressive figure, well over six feet tall, with a strong, ruddy face. He told me to sit down and give him a detailed report of my encounter with the Russians. A shorthand reporter took down everything I said. At the end the general told me to await his return and disappeared through a side door. A few minutes later he came back: General MacArthur wanted to hear my story directly.

It was the first time I had seen Douglas MacArthur in person: an open-necked shirt adorned only by the five-star insignia of his rank on both sides of the collar; the corncob pipe; the thinning hair. He sat behind a large desk. After barely returning my salute, MacArthur said that General Willoughby had given him a summary of my reconnaissance trip to Tsushima, and he now wanted to hear it from my own lips. I reported as concisely as I could. He asked one or two questions. Then he said, "That will be all, lieutenant."

I was dismissed. Not a word of appreciation; in fact, he had never even told me to stand at ease. I looked up an army dentist of my acquaintance who had recently been transferred from Fukuoka to Tokyo and, over lunch with him, I unloaded: It seemed to me that it was not part of the routine duties of a (very) junior artillery staff officer to make a solo jump out of a fighter-bomber into a situation that nobody could assess in advance; some small word of thanks might really have been in order.

But it had also struck me on the way from the Dai-Ichi building that neither MacArthur nor Willoughby had imposed any kind of restrictions on my discussing the incident with others. Much later, when I did some research into events of the occupation of Japan, I learned that only twenty-four hours after my report to MacArthur an American photo reconnaissance plane flew for the first time over Russian-held Port Arthur,[5] the strategically located tip of the Liaotung peninsula, between Korea and the Chinese mainland. Adding two and two

5. Now called Lu'shun.

together, I realized what had happened: If the Russians complained about an American plane over their area of influence, our government could cite my report and assert that the Russian submarine had deliberately violated the American area. Pawns may think that their moves are important on the chessboard, but they are still only pawns.

In between these moments of adventure and excitement life in Fukuoka (and later on the Hakata peninsula) was rather pleasant. Occupation duty changed fairly speedily from watching over the Japanese to standing by and honing one's military skills. A regular cycle of training was started, and I took my turn at the duties this involved. The artillery S-2 in a division unit is responsible for the identification of targets and control over the target area. In peacetime this means setting out targets for the guns to shoot at and establishing survey control over the targets so that the accuracy of the firing can be properly judged.

The Japanese had maintained a large artillery training area south of Kurume, and I was told by the S-3, Major Jones, to go down there and prepare the area to be used for firing exercises by our battalions. I found that the target area was the side of a steep mountain range. I instructed the assistant S-2 what kind of survey operations would be necessary and then returned to Fukuoka with a report that the area was entirely suitable for our purposes. Major Jones, however, expressed doubts about this, and, at his urging, the general decided to inspect the area personally, with Jones and me accompanying him.

When General Blanchard saw the target area, he said at once that this simply would not do: One could not carry on firing practice in this kind of terrain. I asked for permission to show that it could be done. I had an easel and some sheets of paper to demonstrate the use of the mountainside as a target area. All that was necessary was that a few conversions be calculated (something I said I could easily do and also teach the respective battalion teams) and these be used in the fire direction centers. Those judging the exercise only had to keep in mind that consulting the conversion table might slow down the calculation of fire commands by a few seconds.

Blanchard said that nothing like that had ever been taught at Fort Sill (the army's artillery school); just where had I learned it? In the Austrian army, I replied (and indeed, given the mountainous terrain in Austria, these kinds of conversions were standard practice for that army's artillery). The general was furious: "The next thing you are going to tell me," he roared, "is that you once served in the Japanese army. I will not have you make a fool of me." I was dumbfounded; surely he knew that I had been born in Austria and had seen service in the Austrian army. But he did not.

When we got back to Fukuoka he called Willie Cover (the adjutant) in and asked to see my records. As Willy told me the story, he just sat there, stared at the form, and said, "I could have sworn the little smart-ass was pulling my leg." That evening he bought me a drink at the bar and apologized. He was that kind of man.

By this time we had already moved out to "Camp Hakata" on the peninsula. Most of us felt that this was not as comfortable a set-up as the hotel in town, but it did have a number of conveniences. The post exchange was fairly well stocked; there was a good bar in the officers' mess; a movie was shown every night; and there was, of course, a decided advantage in being on the same post with the units under our command. And, of course, some families had already arrived; and others were to follow soon.

But I was not to stay there for long. In January 1947, a new policy required the return to the United States of all personnel who had been overseas more than three years. A few days later an order came down from division headquarters that released me from my assignment as of February 4, 1947 (by coincidence the fourth anniversary of the day when I had been told by Lieutenant Early that I was going to "Divarty"), and directed me to report to the replacement depot at Zama, near Yokohama, the site at which all incoming and outgoing "casuals" were processed.

A few days later the chief of police came to our headquarters and, with some flattering remarks, asked me to accept a sixteenth-century sword that had come down in his family. Later Mr. Matsouka, with tears in his eyes, presented me with a beautiful Hakata doll. Since he could ill afford the price of such a present, I asked Mrs. Blanchard to buy me a ham at the newly established base commissary, drove to Matsuoka's shack on the outskirts of town, and left it with his wife. Her eyes tearing, she told me in halting English that her husband had never worked for anyone he admired as much as he did me.

On the evening before my departure there was a grand party in the officers' club for my farewell. Willy Cover acted as toastmaster and told all sorts of tales, mostly with some literary license, about me. Then General Blanchard related the story of our first encounter, on the beach on Leyte, and said more nice things about me than I ever could have expected. I had great difficulty, in my response, keeping my emotions under control. Once this formal part of the evening was over, I walked across the street to the headquarters building and, for the last time and in the dark, sat down at my desk. I do not recall what thoughts went through my mind, but I know that I realized that, whether I stayed in the army or not, this was a turning point. "Headquarters Twenty-fourth Division Artillery" had been my address longer than any other place since Peter Jordanstrasse 28 in Vienna (where my family had lived from 1920 until 1933). Now it would cease to be my home. I was sorry I had to leave.

I will not claim that I spent the time on the train from Fukuoka to Kyoto and then to Yokohama reflecting on my experiences in Japan. Nor did I really think much about my eighteen months as a "victorious occupier" while I was aboard the ship that took me first to Europe and then back to the States. But once I had returned to Virginia the questions came up time and again: "What was it like? What are the Japanese people like? What were your feelings living among a people that you had been fighting so long?" So the following pages should probably be headed "Thinking about Japan while Sipping Mint Juleps." But, neither was all the thinking done while socializing Virginia-style.

In retrospect, I realized that my responses to these questions were, of course, quite atypical. Differing from most of my comrades in arms, I had previously been exposed to peoples of different cultures and different levels of education. The stereotypes that so easily fell from the lips of my fellow-soldiers were basically at odds with the view of mankind that I had acquired as part of my upbringing. The humanistic education I had received in Vienna prevented me from accepting the black-and-white perceptions that others might hold and the official propaganda encouraged.

My wartime experience was also different from that of others. Even among the infantry there were not many who had passed through the kind of hand-to-hand encounter I had faced in New Guinea; nor were there many who had spent time behind the enemy lines, as I had on Leyte. What I had seen and learned in Japan was, in its totality, perhaps also unique. Moreover, differing from not only my friends in the enlisted ranks but also from my fellow officers, I had read a good deal about Japan. In fact, before our unit set out for Japan, General Cort had me give the officers of the command a briefing on the governmental system of Japan, something I was able to do thanks to the comparative government seminar I had taken in 1941–1942 as part of my doctoral studies. But it was also true that the first live Japanese I had ever encountered were the two snipers who rushed at me with fixed bayonets on that trail in the interior of New Guinea. I had killed both of them. Did I kill them because they were Japanese? I did not think so then (and do not now): I suspect that I would have reacted the same way to anyone who threatened my life.

The next live Japanese I encountered, other than those we ambushed in the interior of New Guinea, were those we took as prisoners after the fighting ended in the late summer of 1945. They came in groups, mostly in the remnants of the military organizations to which they belonged. They did not speak unless they were spoken to, and what we said to them was in the form of orders and directives, not conversation. They looked and acted dejected and somber. I do not remember that I identified any of them, either by name or face.

Almost twenty-five years later my wife and I were in Amsterdam's Schiphol Airport, waiting for a connecting flight that was to take us back to the United States. One of Donna's favorite pastimes was "people watching," and, whenever we were in a public place, she liked to position herself so that she could see as many people as possible. She had done so again this time while I was standing with my back to the interior of the large hall. We were in these relative positions when she told me that a man of Oriental appearance had been staring at me for several minutes. She suggested that I turn slowly and look at him. I did so, and, indeed, there stood a very well dressed man fixing me with his Oriental eyes. When he realized that he had been caught staring, he marched over to us, made a very proper Japanese-style bow and, addressing me in perfect English, apologized for his impolite behavior. He was, he said, quite certain that he and I had met before.

Had I ever been to Tokyo? I told him that I had spent only one day there (at the time of my report to General Willoughby and General MacArthur, after the episode of the Russian submarine in the Tsushimas). I had, then, been in Japan? Yes, I replied, in Okayama, Himeji, and Fukuoka between September 1945 and February 1947. He had not been in any of those places in those years. Then another thought seemed to cross his mind: Where had I been before I came to Japan? The Philippines, I told him. Where in the Philippines? Leyte, Mindoro, Mindanao, I answered. Suddenly a big smile came over his face: "Now I know who you are," he said. "You are the American officer to whom I handed my sword when my unit came into the American lines on Mindanao to surrender." My reply was that, to my regret, I had no recollection of him at all. He insisted that I take his card, bowed to us, and, evidently greatly relieved that he had solved his puzzle, returned to his original place.

What I do not know is whether he understood why I did not remember him, whether he appreciated that, while for him I personified a critical moment in his life, for me he was merely one of hundreds who passed me, and the moment was only one of many that for me made up the end of the war. I am inclined to think that he may have understood that, if for no other reason than the strong tradition among the Japanese that every person should always know his or her place.

Bushido, the code of the Japanese warrior class, has often been compared with European forms of feudalism, and there certainly are many similarities. Most important, each system assumed that, in order to produce optimal conditions of life, society must be stable, and stability can best be attained under hierarchic conditions. You fight a war, and if you are defeated you accept the fact that you are now one of the vanquished: hence that incongruous sign that greeted us at the Okayama railroad station: "Welcome Victorious Occupiers." We laughed about that sign, but it was no more than a message of acknowledgment of the relationship the Japanese people now accepted: "We are the inglorious losers, you are the glorious winners. So be it, welcome! Don't expect us to shed any tears."

Once it was clear that the occupation troops had not come to rape and pillage, the initial sullenness quickly gave way to ready smiles. Our young soldiers made friends among Japanese of their age, many of whom had lost their fathers in the war or, at least, did not know whether they were still alive. The small guard detachment stationed at the general's residence in Okayama thus had made friends with several nearby Japanese families, and one day Jimmy Clanton, the general's orderly, asked me to meet one of these families. The mother had been unable to learn of her husband's whereabouts and thought that she might at least discover from an American officer where she should address her inquiries. I told Jimmy that I would drop by but only for a few minutes.

I do not remember the woman's name, but she was obviously educated, spoke decent English, and her home gave every indication that these were people of some standing and prosperity. She apologized profusely for imposing on me, but it had been nearly a year since she had last heard from her husband. He had been stationed on Mindanao, and she understood that this was where we had been before we came to Japan. I confirmed that fact but also suggested that, since there were over 20,000 of us and more than 75,000 of them, the likelihood that I would be able to tell her anything was miniscule. But I did ask her if she knew his unit designation.

"Yes," she replied, "it was the 144th Independent Mixed Brigade." She named one of the few Japanese units that I did know about. There had been two IMB's, units that, when at full strength, numbered about 8,000 men, that had been dug in on the east flank of Mount Apo. They were among the major targets when we conducted our artillery fire from the bell tower at the hemp factory near our beach encampment. Day after day, some of us (me included) were up in that tower calling for salvo after salvo until in the end there was no sign of any activity. When our infantry eventually reached the area, no survivors were found. One of the two units we had so annihilated was the 144th Independent Mixed Brigade.

What was I to tell the woman? I do not know how long it took me to decide that I could not lie to her. I told her that I was quite certain that there were no survivors of the 144th IMB; *if* (and I stressed that word) her husband had been with his unit in the final weeks of the fighting, he had been among the fallen. I also told her that I had been among those who had personally directed the artillery fire that destroyed the 144th. She showed no emotion but only bowed and thanked me. I excused myself and hurried back to the house where I shared quarters with the general.

This had been much worse than killing those two soldiers in New Guinea. But the next day Jimmy Clanton brought me a small plant from the woman which, he said, she had asked him to take to me as an expression of thanks for "having freed her of great uncertainty." Now she knew, so I would later come to appreciate, what her role and her place were.

A much less poignant but equally telling episode occurred a little later. General Cort had indicated to the Japanese liaison officer that he would like to visit the one large steel factory in our area that had remained fully operational. It was about ten miles outside of Okayama, and the original plan was for the general to make the trip by car (a mode of transportation which he much preferred to flying in a small plane). Then something came up, and he decided that he would go to the site by car but have Lieutenant Erickson bring his Piper Cub to fly him back while I would ride back in the car (with our Japanese driver and Tom, the interpreter). Neither he nor I thought it necessary to tell the Japanese about these plans.

We were met at the entrance of the plant's main building by an array of executives and managers. Introductions were properly made, and then the general, his aide, and his interpreter were escorted to a conference room. There were two rows of tables: each had a center table that seated one and was flanked by two tables that seated three persons each. There were two cushions behind the general for Okamoto and myself; lesser managers of the plant and an interpreter were in a line behind the general manager, and as they seated themselves it was very clear that each of the Japanese knew exactly where his place was. Tea was brought in, and, after the appropriate interval, the general manager made a presentation, his translator providing the English version.

We had carried on like this for about an hour when I heard the plane overhead. Shortly afterward the door to the conference room was opened, and in strode Lieutenant Erickson. To put it mildly, Erickson was a maverick. He was rarely in proper uniform and used the remote location of the airfield as an excuse to avoid all sorts of assignments that did not interest him. Flying was his one love in life. When he flew he favored a combination of clothing that bore little resemblance to anything military. Most important, he wore no insignia of rank.

He took one quick look around, pulled a cushion to the table and seated himself next to the general. Hugh Cort grinned and explained that "his driver" had arrived. Tom Okamoto duly conveyed that information to our host. There was a flurry of whispered exchanges on their side of the table. Tom later told me that the general manager had asked those nearest to him what he should do: One could not have a chauffeur at a management conference, or was this deliberate on the part of the

Americans, to display their famous democratic attitude? General Cort was puzzled and asked the interpreter what was going on. When Tom told him what seemed to concern the Japanese, the general instructed him to explain that Erickson was not a driver, that he was a pilot, and that the general had used the word *driver* jokingly. But the general also sensed that our hosts did not consider it proper for anyone other than the top man in each group to be seated directly at the table, and so he told Erickson to move his cushion next to mine. The air was cleared.

Tom and I talked about the incident on the way to Okayama. He told me that one of the most difficult things he had to get used to in his student days at the University of Oregon was what he thought of as a lack of social structure. He lived in a boardinghouse and could never quite understand why he did not have a fixed place at the table or why everyone just reached for the food instead of following a set order. The way he had been brought up, if one did not know one's place in whatever group one belonged to, one was, in effect, an outcast.

But the longer I was in Japan and the more I saw of Japanese people, the more I came to recognize that it was not merely a matter of having a place but also of knowing one's place. At first, this posed a problem for me, mainly in light of what I had been taught about the nature of government and politics in imperial Japan. Power in that society, so the books said, derived from access to the emperor's person. The fact that the ministers in charge of the army and navy could bypass the prime minister and address the monarch directly meant that the military could not only block any policy proposed by the ostensible head of the government (the prime minister), but that they could actually pursue policies of which he totally disapproved. That this was an invitation to every form of intrigue and backstabbing was borne out by the country's history, its most remarkable example, of course, being the manner in which the shoguns had, for centuries, isolated the emperor from any direct contact with the outside world and thus made themselves de facto rulers of the realm.

There is a great deal of violence in the history of Japan. But it is violence that falls into one of two quite distinct categories: criminal activity by outlaws, and violence perpetrated in accordance with established norms and traditions. One of the sights that fascinated me in Japan was that of persons being escorted by two uniformed policemen to a court of law; they wore formal but simple kimonos, and baskets the size of large beehives covered their heads. These were criminal defendants being taken to trial, but their identities were carefully concealed. I do not know whether this is still done, but the point is that it again underscores the importance of place in the society: There is no justification for exposing the accused to public derision or obloquy as long as his place, guilty or innocent, has not been determined.

This struck me over and over again, the need for understanding where one stood within society at large but also within any of its subgroups. This may well have been General MacArthur's major achievement, that he understood the importance of allowing that preoccupation with structure and place to continue. The well-known picture of MacArthur with Emperor Hirohito, the emperor in morning coat and winged collar and MacArthur in an open-necked shirt but towering over the other, probably had more symbolic value than any orders he issued or any words he spoke.

As I have noted before, I had picked up some street-Japanese, but I never learned to read Japanese script. Just how difficult a task this would be I found out from my old school friend Otto Eiselsberg. Otto, a career diplomat, had served as the Austrian ambassador in Tokyo for four years (1967–1971). He was between marriages and decided to use his spare time to study the language of his host country. At the end of this four-year effort he concluded that "neither the Japanese nor the Chinese will ever give up their script and replace it with that of Western Europe. Their letters significantly affect their thought processes and are indicative of their mental processes."[6]

6. Otto Eiselsberg, *Erlebte Geschichte 1917–1997* (Vienna: Bohlau Verlag, 1997), 295, my tranlation.

12

Around the World in Sixty Days

The military train for Kyoto and Tokyo was due to leave Fukuoka around 2:00 A.M. I had asked Erickson, who had become my roommate after we moved to Camp Hakata, to check out a jeep and drive me to the station, but, to my surprise, when I came out of the officers' quarters building, there was Colonel Walters with the general's sedan. He chauffeured me into the city, about a dozen jeeps following behind us, each with two or three officers in them. They serenaded me until the train had pulled out of the station.

Shortly after daybreak the train arrived in Kyoto. Hugh Cort met me at the station and drove me to his home. I spent three days with him, his wife, and their daughter, Georgia (son Hugh Jr. was in Germany, in the army). They treated me as if I were a part of the family. Then it was on to Yokohama and the Zama Replacement Center.

As I finished checking in at Zama I was stopped by a sergeant who said that he had a message for me: I was to report that afternoon at 2:00 P.M. to Colonel Hardy, at a building and office indicated. When I asked what this was all about, the sergeant said that he did not know but that there were messages with similar instructions for several officers due to report into the center that day. Colonel Hardy was a thickset, gruff individual[1]

1. Since he turned out to be an army edition of Captain Queeg, I do not use his real name.

who shook my hand, told me to have a seat, and announced that he was glad that I had volunteered for "the assignment." I replied with what I hoped was appropriate respect that, to the best of my knowledge, I had not volunteered and did not know anything about the assignment. The colonel grinned and said that it really did not make any difference; I was on his list, and that made me a member of his team: I would be part of the army complement on the *Marine Jumper*, a ship that would take German repatriates from Japan back to Germany. I should be ready from the next day on for a move on short notice to Uraga, our point of embarkation.

When we assembled the following morning for the short trip to Uraga there were eight of us: a lieutenant colonel of military police who had been with First Corps headquarters (and knew Hugh Cort); four majors, of whom one (a West Pointer) had been with the First Cavalry Division, one with the Eleventh Airborne Division, one with the Ninth Corps signal office, and one, a medical officer, with a general hospital in Tokyo; a captain who had been with the Twenty-fifth Infantry Division; and two lieutenants, one who had been with an independent engineer brigade, and I. The medical officer, having been stationed in Tokyo, was the only one who knew why we had been selected for this detour on our way home.

In January there had been a shipment of German repatriates for which Eighth Army headquarters selected the officers in the accompanying detachment. The officer assigned to choose the personnel saw the trip as an attractive fringe benefit and promptly picked himself and eight friends of his, all from Eighth Army headquarters. There had been complaints about this loaded selection procedure; thus, as plans were made for the second shipment, MacArthur's headquarters had directed that the officers chosen should be those who, in each of the major troop units, had the longest time overseas. This was what had landed my name on Colonel Hardy's list (he himself qualified as the person at any of the installations directly under Eighth Army who had been overseas the longest).

Before our "charges" were to arrive we spent several days at Uraga, a former Japanese naval substation. The army detachment there loaned us a truck, and we used the time to visit some of the sights in the vicinity. We saw the shrine at Kamakura, with its giant statue of Buddha, and the monument marking the spot where Commodore Perry had landed in 1854 (and it struck us that, the war notwithstanding, it had obviously been taken care of throughout the years), drove as far up Mount Fuji as the winter snow would allow, and spent a day in Tokyo. Meanwhile the enlisted complement arrived, about fifty men, of whom roughly a third were medical corps personnel and the rest military police. (We also had four nurses and two Red Cross workers on the ship, but they boarded directly, without the layover in Uraga.)

At last our German passengers arrived, about one thousand of them, mostly women and children. There were also somewhat fewer than two hundred men, the crews from four German submarines that had been in Far Eastern waters when the war in Europe ended and, in keeping with international law, had then been interned by the Japanese. They had been held at a remote resort hotel in the mountains above Kobe. Since that was in Hyogo prefecture, which, during our brief stay in Himeji, had been the Twenty-fourth Division Artillery's responsibility, I had known of them and had in fact once visited the hotel that was their internment site. Again as set by international law, these men were now prisoners of war under our control, and as such the enlisted men could be required to perform work. Colonel Hardy promptly advised the senior officer that the U-boat crews would be responsible for the general cleanliness of the returnees' quarters and would also serve as kitchen help.

I had not only greeted the senior German captain by his rank and name but had done so in his language. That was the first time that Colonel Hardy knew that I spoke German. Apparently nobody had considered it necessary that there be somebody aboard who could speak the passengers' language; the assumption was that enough of them would have some knowledge of English so as to make an interpreter unnecessary.

It turned out that one of our enlisted men, a sergeant with the medical detachment, was also a native speaker of German. He and I became the links in the communication between the Germans and the ship's company and the army detachment. Colonel Hardy later commented that on the first shipment there had been mostly businessmen and their families; many of them did indeed speak English. But on this second shipment we had a preponderance of families of missionaries, teachers, and small traders. They spoke Japanese but rarely knew much English. Among the naval personnel only a few of the officers had even limited knowledge of English.

There was one exception to this generalization, and this was a man who obviously was well connected. He and his family did not go through Uraga but were brought to our ship on a sloop, escorted by a colonel from MacArthur's headquarters and accompanied by the major who was to travel with us as the senior nurse (and, so it was rumored, had been the colonel's girlfriend). The German family were placed in two adjoining cabins on the main deck; all other Germans were in large holds below. The ostensible reason for this favored treatment was that the two sons of the family had been born in the United States and therefore had to be treated as American citizens and should not be separated from their family. The man was arrogant and overbearing, and neither the other Germans aboard nor the rest of us had much use for the privileged quartet.

Our own accommodations were relatively comfortable. The ship's cabins were equipped to accommodate junior officers on a troop transport. Each cabin had three canvas bunks, one above the other; for our voyage each of the officers had a cabin to himself. This made it possible to unpack one's belongings and arrange them on two of the bunks and use the third one as a bed. For every two cabins there was a shower bath. What was lacking were tables and chairs and a place where one might be able to hang up a uniform.

Our contingent of enlisted men did not have quite the same amount of space, but each man had an extra bunk, and for every four men there was a shower bath. Our German passengers were housed in two large areas—women and small children in one, men in the other. Fortunately, their own sense of orderliness caused them to keep the areas, which otherwise might easily have turned filthy, reasonably clean. This was particularly important since they had to take their meals in the same area and washing facilities were limited. The *Marine Jumper* had not been intended for passengers' comfort.

For us mealtime meant the dining room used by the ship's officers, and our enlisted men ate with the ship's crew. The men also had the use of the crew's recreation room just as the officers were welcome to use the ship's officers' lounge. The junior officers (all three of us) took turns serving as officers of the guard while the majors rotated officer-of-the-day duty among themselves. Fortunately, for much of the voyage the weather was decent so that both Germans and Americans could spend much of their time on deck. The other facilities were, for all, rather cramped. I counted seven children, several obviously ill, all of them visibly undernourished. It was a stark lesson in human misery.

The following day our new passengers were brought on board. Included in this group were seventeen men who had been convicted by an allied military court in Shanghai as war criminals. This was the "Gruppe Erhard," a team of specialists in various intelligence activities (mostly demolition and intelligence) who had been loaned by the German government to the Japanese army for use in China. Their offense was that they continued to give their services to the Japanese after Germany had surrendered (i.e., they had continued as belligerents after their government had signed its instrument of surrender).[2] These men were housed in a separate area of the ship and were allowed on deck only for two one-hour periods a day, and then always under guard. The other passengers who came aboard here impressed us by the fact that they were much better dressed and carried much better luggage than did the passengers from Japan: They were all professional men and their families; most of them had spent their years in the Far East in Shanghai.

One additional passenger who joined us in Shanghai did not come up the gangplank: One of the German women gave birth to a baby boy. Years afterward I was asked to verify this birth because the young man involved was trying to establish his citizenship status: As son of a Japanese father (who did not accompany the family to Germany), he was a Japanese; as son of a German mother, he was a German; having been born under the American flag, he had a potential claim to American citizenship; and because the ship was tied up in Chinese waters, he also had a potential claim to Chinese citizenship. He had raised this question at the time of his induction into the army of the Federal Republic of Germany and the German defense ministry referred it to the American liaison officer on duty with the ministry.

2. The convictions of the members of the "Gruppe Erhard" were eventually upheld by the Supreme Court of the United States. *Johnson v. Eisentrager*, 339 U.S. 763 (1950).

That happened to be my brother Tom. When he saw the ship's name (*Marine Jumper*), he remembered that this was the ship I had been on and sent the question on to me. (I was not much help to the young man: So much time had elapsed that only his claims to German and Japanese citizenship claims were still valid.)

From Shanghai we sailed southward and then turned west toward our next stop, Singapore. Again, while the ship took on provisions, we had the opportunity to go ashore, although this time for only a few hours, just long enough to take a short tour through the center of the city and have a couple of drinks in the bar of the famed Raffles Hotel.

The next leg of our voyage took us to Colombo, Ceylon (now Sri Lanka). The approach into the harbor of Colombo was impressively beautiful. When we got ashore, the city was no less attractive. Ceylon is famous for its gemstones, and Colonel Hardy was eager to buy some. So one of our first stops was at a gem shop. I had never seen anything like it: After the dealer had ascertained what kind of stones the colonel was interested in (sapphires), he disappeared behind a curtain and shortly came out with a felt-lined tray and a large velvet bag. He emptied the contents of the bag into the tray; there must have been two hundred uncut sapphires of all sizes and description. He would reach in with a gloved hand and fish out a stone that he would hold up against a light for inspection. The colonel bought a star sapphire about the size of a thumbnail and paid $600 for it.

Later, as we were having a drink in the bar of the Grand Hotel, a man in a white tropical suit came over and introduced himself as a buyer for Tiffany's, the famous New York City jewelry store. He had been in the store at the same time and congratulated the colonel on his purchase. The colonel asked him how much a ring made with this stone might sell for back in the States. The answer, said the man, was fairly simple: As a regular buyer for a major American jewelry firm he would probably have gotten the stone for less than the colonel had paid, perhaps $500. Tiffany would have given him twice that, $1,000. Preparation of the stone and setting it in a ring would probably cost Tiffany about one fourth of that, bringing the cost to Tiffany to $1,250. And Tiffany would probably put it for sale at twice that amount, $2,500. Colonel Hardy was elated.

Actually, most of us had by this time taken a decided dislike to the colonel who had shown himself in a variety of ways to be arbitrary, unreasonable, and utterly selfish. On the next leg of our trip, which took us to Suez, life with Colonel Hardy came to be very uncomfortable. Personally my most unpleasant episode came one evening when he had asked me to play cribbage with him and I had beaten him decisively. It was the first time in my several years of cribbage playing that I had scored the maximum number of points, 29; it would not happen again for 47 years! As a result I "double-skunked" him: When I finished the board with its 121 points, he had fewer than sixty points and had to pay me four times the sum (which wasn't very large) we were playing for. He threw the board and the cards against the bulkhead and screamed about the indecency of junior officers who did not know on which side their bread was buttered.

Shortly after we had left Colombo, the colonel decided that he was not satisfied with the security aboard ship. He had lost (or misplaced) a pair of dark glasses, but claimed that they had been stolen. He ordered the number two man, the MP lieutenant colonel from First Corps, to make a thorough investigation. After two days, the military police officer reported that he was satisfied that there had been no theft. The colonel relieved him of his duties as executive officer of the detachment and said he would supervise security himself. He doubled the guards and required the officer of the guard to be on duty and awake for twenty-four hours a day. He started inspecting the officers' cabins randomly and unannounced. He regularly attended guard mount and often personally inspected the guard. One day he happened to come across one of the officers talking with one of the German women: he had him placed under arrest and prepared court-martial charges against him. Increasingly he reminded me of General Archbold (and, later, the *Caine Mutiny*'s infamous Captain Queeg). The other officers seemed to feel the same. The West Pointer reached the conclusion that he did not want to stay in the army; I concluded that, while I would have liked to serve with officers like Hugh Cort, Tommy Lang, Livy Taylor, and Max Pitney, an army with Archbolds and Hardys was not where I wanted to spend my life. The major from the Eleventh Airborne who, like me, had applied for a Regular Army commission, arrived at the same conclusion.

The two majors and I were lucky enough to win the draw when, upon the ship's arrival at Suez, three officers were allowed to leave the ship, go to Cairo, and then rejoin the ship at Port Said. It was on this trip (which we made by taxi) that we talked at length about Hardy and confirmed our conclusions not to stay in or enter the regular service.

We were able to include a visit to the pyramids in this trip, and I found them even more impressive in reality than in the many pictures of them I had seen since my early childhood interest in discoveries and explorations. In Cairo we stayed at Shephard's, another famous hotel which, a few years later, would be burned to the ground, this in the course of the uprisings that led to the expulsion of King Fu'ad and the establishment of republican (albeit not democratic) government in Egypt.

Our crossing of the Mediterranean brought us the first bad weather we had experienced; after we had passed Gibraltar and were sailing northward in the Atlantic, we passed through two successive severe storms. Our passengers, unable to go on deck during the day, were miserable. I spent a good deal of my time in their area, trying to reassure women and children who had never experienced this kind of adversity. But their morale did not really improve until we had entered the English Channel and they could see land. At long last, thirty-three days after we had left Japan, the ship docked in Bremerhaven.

Since it was the duty of our detachment to deliver the Germans to their destinations in Germany, we boarded the train that was waiting for them (and us). It took us through Hanover and Frankfurt to Ludwigsburg near Stuttgart, which was the reception center for repatriates from overseas. All along the train's route, the extent of the destruction that had been wrought on Germany was starkly evident. The huge railroad station in Frankfurt was a skeleton of twisted steel girders. When, at last, we spent a few days in Stuttgart in one of the few remaining hotels, the piles of rubble outside reached so high that the only way to enter the hotel was over a second-story balcony.

Before we had these few days in Stuttgart, however, two of the majors, the engineering lieutenant, and I, along with some of the men from our guard detachment, delivered the group of convicted war criminals that we had picked up in Shanghai at Dachau near Munich. A part of this huge and notorious concentration camp had been moderately cleaned up and was being used to hold such prisoners until they could be placed in permanent prison facilities. After we had turned them over to the American camp personnel, we were given a tour of the former concentration camp. There were, of course, none of the displays that in later years would remind visitors of the horrors that had been perpetrated there, but our guide did not spare us the verbal descriptions. In one barracks, there was a long table on which there were molding piles of the striped prison garb worn by the inmates. I looked at my American army uniform and reflected that, but for the providence that, back in the spring of 1938, led my classmate to warn me that I was about to be arrested by the Gestapo, I would have worn one of these shredding prison uniforms and might well have died in Dachau or some place like it.

After the brief sojourn in Stuttgart, most of us returned to Bremerhaven where we were pleased to find that we were to reboard the *Marine Jumper*; we were given the same accommodations that we had had before which gave us more space and better eating facilities than were available to the officers who boarded the ship here for the first time. Filled to capacity with GIs returning to the States (and a small group of British and French war brides), the ship sailed for the United States. A week later we docked at Staten Island. We were taken by bus to Fort Dix, New Jersey, where two days later I was released from active duty. As part of the procedure, I gladly signed a form accepting transfer to the U.S. Army Reserve.

13 Reprise

Fort Bragg Again

As a civilian my highest priority was getting a Ph.D. completed. Sometime during the summer the military drew my attention with a telegram from the War Department advising me that I had been appointed a second lieutenant in the Regular Army, the rank to date from the message's date. It came to me how pleased Hugh Cort would be. But I turned it down. My adverse experiences with Colonel Hardy had something to do with my decision but mainly it was chronology that determined it.

In a few weeks I would be thirty years old, but the rank being offered me would place me behind all officers graduated (presumably at the age of twenty-two or twenty-three) from the military academy, ahead only of future officers. Aside from wartime promotions (and in 1947 practically nobody expected early war) there was little for me to expect in the Regular Army.

In the year that followed I gave all my efforts to preparation for a life as an academic. I received my doctoral degree in June 1948 and later that summer was appointed, for one year, as an assistant professor of political science at the University of Kansas. The best of this was that I could teach an undergraduate class in constitutional law and that, among seventy students, there were several who took on lasting importance in my life, foremost among them Donna Concannon Munn, who, a year later, became my wife.

One student who was an influence on me, though he was not in my constitutional law class, was William Gaw, about to graduate in architecture. He introduced himself to me as the commanding officer of a reserve artillery battery that had just been started up in town and asked if I would be interested in joining his unit. In light of his impending graduation I could expect to succeed him in command of the battery. This would be more time than other possible reserve duties (the battery trained once a week), but there was pay for it. By summer I was the battery commander and six months later was promoted to captain.

That summer of 1949 I spent at Fort Leavenworth, largely through the intervention of George Baxter Smith, the dean of the School of Education, who had reached the rank of full colonel as a general staff officer in the European theater and had ties to the U.S. Army's Command and General Staff College (C&GSC) in Leavenworth. Smith knew that the C&GSC was at that time eager to have faculty members of civilian institutions who were also reserve officers come on short tours of active duty and take on various assignments related to the preparation of the courses the college was teaching. I served on active duty that summer for nearly three months and would do so again the following year; my connection with C&GSC, for a dozen years in a military capacity and later on as a civilian adviser, would not end until 1975.

In the summer of 1950, after I had completed my active duty at Fort Leavenworth, I took my own reserve unit, Battery A of the 758th Field Artillery Battalion, to Camp McCoy, Wisconsin, for the required two weeks of summer training. This was my first opportunity to meet any of the rest of the battalion.

The battalion commander, Cecil Coffey, a rather pudgy man, was a bank cashier in Kansas City, Kansas. He had been in the National Guard and had seen wartime service in the Aleutians but not in the artillery. The executive officer, Maj. Frank Tainter, and some of the captains had experience as battery commanders or battery executive officers, but I was the only one with staff experience. Since the number of enlisted men was so small that we really could not field more than one firing section, Colonel Coffey asked me to take over all the administrative staff functions during summer camp. It was not particularly stimulating, but at least I had the opportunity to get to know some of my counterparts, and while they were not exactly exciting either, some became good friends and valued associates.

Earlier that summer, while I was at Fort Leavenworth, the country (and the world) had been startled when North Korea invaded South Korea. There was, of course, a good deal of discussion at Camp McCoy of what this might mean for our reserve unit. Colonel Coffey had already been advised that there would be a workshop for unit commanders at the state capital in Topeka in September to review the procedures that would apply if a reserve unit were to be called to active duty. But Coffey had also been informed that at that moment the army saw no need for "very heavy" artillery units. Except for me, none of us had ever seen anything but light and medium artillery; the 758th, on paper, was a 240mm howitzer unit, and the 240 was the heaviest artillery piece the United States Army then had. We would go to the workshop, but all the signs indicated that we would not be called.

But six months later the call came. My wife, Donna, and I were in her hometown, Garden City, in western Kansas, for the university's spring vacation. On about the third evening there we were playing bridge at the home of one of Donna's cousins when the phone rang. The call was for me: It was Jim Bailey, my executive officer in Battery A. He had just been informed by Colonel Coffey that the 758th Field Artillery Battalion had been called to active duty and was to report to Fort Bragg, North Carolina, on May 1. He, Bailey, I, and three non-commissioned officers of my choice were to go on active duty on April 1 to get the unit ready for the move.

I cannot say that I was either surprised or dismayed by this turn of events. Of course, when I signed up for the army reserve in June 1947, nobody expected that there would be an early need to call on the reserves. But once the Korean War had started in June 1950, it was plausible that this might happen, and while I was not eager to go, neither did I feel any resentment or regret. I had, after all, agreed to be available.

The timing was not the best, to be sure. At the annual meeting of the American Political Science Association the Christmas past, I had been approached by the chair of the department at the University of Illinois who invited me to become a candidate for their position in the subfield of public law. Illinois was a very good department, perhaps not among those ranked at or near the top but very good. It certainly enjoyed wider repute than the department at Kansas, and the Illinois public law position had a certain aura: Over the past sixty years it had been held by only three persons, each of them a nationally recognized scholar in the field. The last in the sequence, John Mathews, was due to retire at the end of the academic year, and the department was searching for a suitable younger person to take his place.

I had been to Champaign for an interview which, I felt, had gone well. Before too long I was informed that the choice had been narrowed to just two persons, of which I was one. The other, I quickly discovered, was Jack Peltason, a 1947 Princeton Ph.D. One of the first things I did after I received the call from Jim Bailey was to call Peltason and tell him that the field was his.[1]

When we returned to Lawrence, I talked to Ethan Allen, the chairman of the political science department, and we made arrangements for my section of the basic course to be taken over by a graduate student. My colleague Hilden Gibson agreed to teach the remaining portion of my course on Far Eastern governments and politics after my departure from Lawrence. The third course (constitutional law) we decided to accelerate, and I continued to teach it (in uniform, of course) through the month of April, at which point it was cut off.

The battery commanders met with Colonel Coffey at his home in Kansas City to review what had to be done. Coffey was not exactly pleased with the prospect of active duty. He did not know why the 758th had been chosen (and would not discover the ostensible reason for our call-up until quite a while after we had arrived at Fort Bragg). During our discussion we realized that we were woefully deficient in the qualifications of our officers. None of them had ever attended the advanced course at the artillery school (and I, of course, had never attended *any* military school, there or anywhere else). As was to be expected, our new bosses at Fort Bragg, the Fifth Corps Artillery headquarters,[2] had spotted this shortcoming and, when we came under their control upon our arrival, they informed Colonel Coffey that Major Tainter, the executive officer, would report to Fort Sill within a week for the advanced course.

1. Peltason went on to a succession of impressive leadership positions in higher education, including the presidencies of the University of California and the American Council on Education.

2. Fifth Corps (where I met Paul Keating again) was in the process of moving to Germany and to be replaced by the Eighteenth Airborne Corps.

This made Capt. J. R. "Bob" Jennings the senior officer after the colonel and thus placed him in the position of executive officer. As soon as Tainter returned from Fort Sill, Jennings would depart to take the same course. Colonel Coffey shifted me from the command of Battery A (which Jim Bailey took over) to battalion headquarters to serve as S-3 (operations and training officer) until both Tainter and Jennings would again be available.

The army wasted no time. Within two weeks new officers had arrived to bring us to about 75 percent of authorized strength, and a week later we received a large assignment of newly inducted draftees, for whom we were to conduct the traditional thirteen weeks of basic training. Fortunately we also received about thirty experienced noncommissioned officers, including a master sergeant to assist me in the S-3 office. He was a rather disagreeable character, but he knew what was expected of him and, between the two of us, we managed to get the training cycle under way and, eventually, completed.

At about the time the training cycle ended, we were told that the battalion would have to furnish the post guard for two nonconsecutive weeks during the next month. The post area of Fort Bragg was virtually denuded of troops as the Third Army staged a major, monthlong maneuver on the huge range area west of the post. Only the 758th and a battalion of maintenance engineers were not involved and were therefore available to furnish the guard.

Each day that we had to furnish the guard, we had to supply more than a hundred men, with a captain as post officer of the day and three lieutenants as officers in charge of each shift of guards. There were only four captains present for duty in our battalion, and one, the adjutant, was not available for duty as officer of the day. That meant that I found myself as commander of the post guard two or three times during each of the four weeks involved.

One of the duties of the post officer of the day was to count the prisoners in the post stockade three times: in the evening, in the middle of the night when they were in their bunks, and at reveille. The stockade was an eye-opener for me. Prisoners who, for whatever infraction of the prison's discipline, were in solitary confinement were literally kept caged, stark naked, in cells with steel floors and without any furnishings whatsoever. The manner in which the guards handled the prisoners was brutal to the extreme. I saw prisoners beaten because they were not standing sufficiently erect in the formation, and, on at least two occasions, I saw the guards use whips on prisoners.[3] And this was a prison for *minor* offenders, those serving six months or less. Fortunately, this sort of military confinement facility no longer exists.

My last tour of duty coincided with the end of the maneuver. Around 2:00 A.M. I received a call from the officer in charge of the officers' club who said that he was being prevented from closing the club at its regular hour by a large number of inebriated officers. I put thirty men into three trucks, got into my jeep, and went to the club. In the fountain outside the club, about a dozen, more or less naked men were having a water fight. Inside, the scene was chaotic. The club officer's main concern was that at both bars the regular bartenders had been driven away by some of the drunken officers who were dispensing booze freely to one and all.

I went back outside, had the men in the trucks dismount, and told the sergeant in charge to enter the building through the rear entrance; I would give him a signal when I wanted him to bring the men in and begin to push the occupants of the club toward the main doors. I called the guardhouse and had one of the lieutenants bring six more trucks, plus an additional thirty men. Once they had arrived, I went out on the stage with a bullhorn in hand and ordered everyone to leave; those who would not do so peacefully, I announced, would be removed forcibly and taken to the post guardhouse. It worked better than I expected; we did not have to arrest more than about two dozen, including the chief of staff of one of the divisions that had come to Bragg for the maneuver. The post commander wrote me a letter commending me for my handling of the situation (and the colonel I had arrested sent me an apology for his conduct).

In all this time, Donna had not been with me. She had remained in Lawrence to complete work on a graduate certificate in social work but was due to join me in August. What few belongings we had had already been shipped by the army into dead storage in Fayetteville (the nearest city to Fort Bragg) while we would sublease the furnished quarters of an

3. My orders specifically stated my authority was limited to the prison's security. I could not issue orders to the guards.

officer who had been assigned to temporary duty elsewhere. It was on the very day that Donna was scheduled to arrive that I found out what the army had in store for the 758th.

Colonel Coffey and I had been ordered to report to the general commanding the corps artillery. General Wood advised us that the information he was about to give us was highly classified and was not to be discussed with anyone. The army, he told us, had developed a large gun capable of delivering a missile with an atomic warhead. Two battalions would be equipped with this new weapon, a 280mm cannon mounted like a fire department's hook-and-ladder unit. The 758th would be one of these "atomic cannon" battalions. The battalion commander (Colonel Coffey) and I, as S-3, would be sent to White Sands Proving Ground in New Mexico for three weeks to receive classified instruction on the new weapon.

Colonel Coffey asked why the 758th had been selected for this task. Simple, the general replied: The 758th is a "very heavy" outfit, and, obviously, a 280mm cannon is a very heavy weapon. It did not seem to me (and even more to Colonel Coffey) a "simple" matter that we should now get this "super cannon." But what we thought about this decision really did not matter.

Of course, the orders for us to go to New Mexico did not come right away, and Donna and I had about six weeks in the subleased apartment. Then the original tenant was due to return. We found another sublease, moved in, and found that the place needed a total cleaning. In the midst of this effort came my orders: Be ready to leave for White Sands at 8:00 A.M. the following day. We decided that, since I was going be gone for three weeks and out of communication, Donna might as well visit her mother in Kansas. She made arrangements to leave the day after my scheduled departure.

But I never went to White Sands. Colonel Coffey and I had already boarded the army plane that was to take us there when I was told to get my gear, deplane, and report immediately to corps headquarters. There, without any explanation for the change in signals, I was told that I had been placed on detached service with the artillery officer of Third Army to serve as member of a testing team that was to examine the artillery of the Forty-third Infantry Division (a Minnesota National Guard unit) and then perhaps others. I was to report at Camp Rucker, near Dothan, Alabama, where the Forty-third was stationed, in three days.

I stopped by the 758th and asked Major Tainter, the battalion commander in Coffey's absence, what he knew. He said that corps artillery had merely told him that he should not expect me to be available for several months. But he was more concerned about what was going to happen to him and the other officers of the original group. A Regular Army major, senior to him, was due to arrive the following week and would take over command from him. Three captains were due in the following week. Maybe someone in higher headquarters had decided that "the reserves" should be sent to Korea. He was clearly worried and not overly interested in my situation.

I was, after all, the only one of the 758th's officers who was protected against being shipped to Korea: An army regulation provided that anyone who had more than three years in combat overseas in World War II would not be sent to Korea. Perhaps that was all that was behind this special assignment I had been given. (I must confess that I had thought of a different explanation: that some intelligence officer in a higher headquarters had decided that a naturalized citizen was not "safe" to learn about the new secret weapon.)[4]

Actually I found the assignment with the Third Army testing team quite interesting. The task was to observe and evaluate the artillery of the division in question in a variety of tactical situations, both during the day and at night. The team was large enough so that every phase of the exercises could be observed by one or two members of the team. As a captain I was a junior member of the team, and my assignment was usually with the forward observers. That was certainly more to my liking than watching the crew of a fire direction center at work in a crowded (and at night a blacked-out) tent.

Our team, though with shifting membership, examined three divisions, the Forty-third, the Thirty-first (like the Forty-third a National Guard division, in training at Camp Gordon, near Augusta, Georgia) and the 101st Airborne, a Regular Army unit based at Fort Campbell,

4. The atomic cannon was never more than a weapon in psychological warfare. Its initial testing under field conditions revealed that its weight made it virtually impossible to move or to emplace on any surface other than solid concrete. That clearly negated its use in Korea. The 758th was eventually sent to Germany, where it traveled about the country, using Hitler's *Autobahnen*, to display its huge guns to as many Germans as possible, a symbol as it were, but never more, of America's armed might.

Kentucky. It was at Campbell that I got into unexpected trouble.

The observation posts for the firing exercises were located at the extreme western end of the military reservation and were reached by driving clear around the reservation and entering it from the other end, a trip of over an hour each way. On the second or third day that we had done this, my fellow team member, a captain from the Eighty-second Airborne Division, suggested that, since we were running well behind schedule and it was about to get dark, we return to the post by way of what appeared to be a service road that, we could see from our vantage point, ran directly across the southern part of the reservation.

I was driving the jeep the division had given us for the duration of the test, and, since I was just as eager to get back and change into clean clothes as my companion was, I set out on the service road. We were about halfway back to the post. It had gotten dark, and we were traveling through a heavily wooded area, when suddenly I saw a barrier across the road. As I came to a halt, bright, obviously powerful searchlights bore down on us. From somewhere on the other side of the barrier a voice on a loudspeaker or bullhorn ordered us to dismount, leave any weapons we might have in the vehicle, and walk ten steps forward with our hands above our heads. As soon as we had done so we were surrounded by soldiers with submachine guns pointed at us. A sergeant came forward and asked for identification from each of us. I asked what this was all about. He had a question in return: Had I not seen the sign two miles back that directed all traffic to the post to turn south and proceed on the state highway outside the reservation? I allowed that I had seen the sign but had assumed that it had been placed there because of the artillery firing during the day, part of the test which we were here to conduct on behalf of Third Army. That was not the case at all, he told me; this area was permanently off-limits to anyone except specially authorized personnel, and even they were not allowed to approach from the direction we had come.

We pleaded ignorance of post regulations. He said that might well be possible, but he had no choice but to detain us until our story could be checked. So we stood and waited while he called post headquarters, which referred him to division headquarters, which referred him to division artillery headquarters where, at long last, the executive officer confirmed that we were indeed who we said we were. We were allowed to continue on the service road but were escorted by two jeeps, one in front and one behind us, each with armed men, to make sure that we did not stop anywhere until we had gotten beyond the restricted area.

When we got back to the post the executive officer told us that we had, in our ignorance, stumbled on the army's storage area for atomic warheads! (It was soon moved to another location, so I am not revealing any military secrets.)

Between these division tests I always returned to Fort Bragg. Donna was back in Kansas, but my belongings were still at the 758th. I tried to find out what my future assignment might be but was unable to get an answer from anyone, although the second time around, after we had been at Camp Gordon, the new major in command of the 758th told me that I could expect to be transferred to another battalion within the corps artillery. It was near the end of our stay at Fort Campbell that the officer in charge of our team, a lieutenant colonel from Third Army headquarters, told me that he had heard that I had been transferred to the 449th Field Artillery Observation Battalion, also at Fort Bragg.

I knew that the 449th was one of the units in the corps artillery, that it was a North Carolina National Guard outfit, and that it had experienced serious difficulties, both in administrative inspections and tactical training tests. What I had not heard was that it had failed each of these crucial tests not once, but twice and that the corps artillery commander had then recommended to the corps commander that all officers who had originally come on active duty with the unit be transferred out immediately and a new group of captains and field grade officers be assigned to bring the unit up to the required standards. Evidently the situation was so grave that this drastic recommendation was approved. Lt. Col. George Harriss, a West Pointer who had been in command of a battalion in the Eighty-second Airborne Division, had been brought in to take over the battalion, and two majors and six captains, of which I was one, had been transferred in from other units. Because of my commitment to the Third Army testing team I was the last of the new officers to report in. Colonel Harriss gave me a short briefing on the dismal state of the unit and then told me that I was to take over Battery C. It was, he said with a half-smile, the worst of the lot: Nearly half of its men were absent without leave; the former first sergeant was awaiting trial by court-martial for having sold places on the duty roster to the men; the former mess sergeant was also due to be tried, on charges that he had sold meat supplied for the unit on the black market. Colonel Harriss wished me luck.

I walked to the battery area and stepped into the orderly room. Normally, the entrance of an officer of a rank higher than that of any person already present would cause the first person who saw him to call "Attention!" There were three men in the office, two of them with their feet on the clerk's desk, the third stretched out on the floor. Nobody moved. At last the man on the floor asked what he might do for me. I asked if there was an officer present. Still reclining on the floor, he said, yes, there was, a lieutenant. I asked the man for his name and that got him to his feet. "Corporal Jones [not his real name], battery clerk, sir." "I am Captain Heller," I said, "and I am the new battery commander. After I have talked to the lieutenant, report to me, and you can tell me why I should not have you placed on the next shipment to Korea." Suddenly the other two men remembered that they had to be someplace else. I got their names and told them to report to me in an hour.

The lieutenant had heard the commotion, and he came out of the inner office and gave me a halfhearted salute. I introduced myself and said that I wanted the battery to be formed before lunch, at which time he could turn over command to me. He looked at me with a distressed expression on his face and asked if that was really necessary. I told him that it was not necessary but that I considered it desirable. He admitted that he just did not know how to do that. I asked where the first sergeant was (the colonel had told me that a seasoned first sergeant had been assigned to the battery three days earlier); it appeared that the sergeant was moving into his quarters that day. Who was the next senior noncommissioned officer? It turned out to be one of the two men I had caught lounging when I came in. I sent the battery clerk to get him and told him that I wanted all personnel except the cooks on duty at a mandatory formation at 11:45. The battery clerk asked sheepishly where he was to be. I told him to be at the formation: Since the lieutenant would not be taking part, he could remain in the orderly room and answer the phone.

The lieutenant was obviously ready to have me take over. He was, he told me, the last of the battery's original four officers and had just received orders sending him to Korea. That he was scared out of his wits at the prospect of combat duty is putting it mildly. He had been too young for World War II and had received his commission out of ROTC just weeks before the fighting in Korea had started. He knew, he told me, virtually nothing about the duties of a forward observer, yet that was the kind of duty he would have to expect. "I am as good as dead," he wailed.

This dismal conversation was fortunately interrupted by the ringing of the telephone. "Sir," said a firm voice at the other end, "this is First Sergeant Morrison [his real name and I am proud to use it]. I regret that I was not at my place of duty when the captain ["Ah," I said to myself, "an old soldier; this is the way an old-time regular addresses an officer"] came in. I do not have a telephone at my quarters yet, but Corporal Jones sent one of the men down here to let me know that the captain has arrived. I will be in the orderly room in twenty minutes."

Exactly twenty minutes later, he knocked at my door and reported to me. I had guessed right: He was an old-timer, and, once I had told him to sit down, he made it very clear how delighted he was to see me. The colonel had told him at the time he reported to the battalion who his battery commander would be, and he had talked to some of the senior NCO's in the 758th; they had told him that Captain Heller was a "no-nonsense" officer.

The biggest problem, he said, was that, while some of the sergeants were potentially good men, the officers had been so lax that none of the noncoms really knew what was expected of them. Another thing puzzled him: the army had placed this National Guard unit so close to its home base, the coastal town of Morehead City, a mere 130 miles from Fort Bragg, that every weekend there was a veritable exodus of the men, with some of them often not returning on time. I assured him that all of that would change very rapidly. For one, I would personally be at the reveille formation every morning. He was glad to hear that but said I should know that, under the former officers, only the privates and corporals had to be present for that formation, and the battery commander rarely appeared before 8:00 A.M. I told him that I would announce at the pre-lunch formation that, starting immediately, I would be at reveille, and everyone had to be present. He beamed: "Sir, that's the best signal the captain can give them!"

I asked him what shape the unit's equipment was in. He hesitated: "You know, sir, this is no regular artillery outfit— there aren't any guns here—those I know but all sorts of stuff that I have never had anything to do with. So I can only tell you what the platoon and section chiefs have told me. Survey I understand, and it is apparently in good shape, but the radar chief has told me that none of his four units is in working condition. The communications chief strikes me as basically incompetent. The motor sergeant has just been shipped out, and the acting guy is weak. Both have told me that their equipment is in good shape, but I don't trust them on that. The sound-ranging platoon, well, I just don't understand what they are doing and what equipment is critical to them. I imagine the captain knows that the mess sergeant is in the stockade; I think the mess hall is just that, a real mess. But there are some good men around, and I really think the outfit can be turned. The captain can count on me to do whatever is necessary."

I got up and walked around the desk. He was already on his feet. I grasped his hand: "Sergeant Morrison," I said, "those are my orders from the colonel: Turn this outfit around. I mean to do that, and more: Six months from now, C Battery of the 449th will be in the running for the best company-sized unit in the whole Third Army." "You can count on me every step of the road, sir," he replied. I felt a lot better about my new assignment.

I had Corporal Jones come in. He gave me the smartest salute I had seen in a long time. I asked him why I had found him on the floor instead of behind his typewriter and why it had taken him so long to get on his feet and report to me. "Sir," he said, "if I may be allowed to say so, I am not one of the North Carolina boys. I can be a sharp soldier, but nobody before seemed to give a damn. Our former captain told me to call him by his first name. I am a draftee, and I don't plan to stay in the army. But while I'm in, I'll be much happier if things are done right. I'll make you the best damn clerk you ever had, if you'll give me the chance." "Jones," I said, "if there are more men in this outfit with your attitude, we'll make something out of it yet." "Does that mean, sir, that you'll let me keep my job?" "Yes, Jones. I'll work your tail off but you'll never be sorry." Some years ago, Jones sent me an announcement of the birth of his first grandson who, like his father, had been given the middle name Francis.

The initial formation went fairly well. I announced that the same afternoon I would talk to each of the platoon and section chiefs in turn and that, after retreat, I would be available to talk to any of the men who wanted to speak to me. I also announced that I would be present at reveille and that all men not on duty or just coming off night duty were to be present. I dismissed the formation and told Sergeant Morrison to return to his quarters and finish moving in. He was obviously grateful for my suggestion.

In spite of my warning, when reveille was sounded the next morning, some of the sergeants were absent. Sergeant Morrison offered to go through the barracks and roust them out. I told him to remain in his place and instructed the battery clerk to go to the orderly room and announce over the public address system (so that everyone could hear it) that this was the last call for reveille and any man not in the formation within two minutes would face disciplinary action. All but two of the absentees promptly showed up. But I noticed that a number of the men were wearing bedroom slippers, some of them had evidently pulled on their fatigues over their pajamas; it was hardly a unit ready for a day's work. Their expectation, of course, was that, as soon as I had received the first sergeant's report, they would be dismissed and be able to rush (or amble) to breakfast. But I ordered "right face, forward march," then had them break into double time (i.e., start running) and led them around the entire block of the sixteen barracks that housed the battalion. When we returned (and more than half of them had dropped out) I told the men that they had their choice: From now on they would come out for reveille in proper attire or they would run before breakfast, and the distance would increase every day. I also announced that the two sergeants who had missed the formation would be restricted to the battery area for the next two weeks.

Colonel Harriss came by later in the morning and asked how things were going. I told him what I had done so far, and he gave a low whistle. "The way to go, captain," he said. Then he told me that I could expect to have a first lieutenant assigned as my executive officer within the next few days and probably two second lieutenants in two or three weeks. I asked what could be expected to improve the situation with the sergeants. He had asked corps artillery for at least twenty experienced noncommissioned officers to be assigned to the 449th, but so far had not been able to get a firm commitment. If any such men came to the battalion, I would certainly get my share, but every effort should be made to see if some of the present noncoms could be salvaged.

The other thing that concerned him was the AWOL rate. He had already looked at the day's morning reports and had noted (as, of course, had I) that of the 188 men assigned to Battery C, 82 were listed as absent without leave. I called his attention to the fact that, of these

82, close to forty had been carried as AWOL for more than ninety days. Under army regulations, these men could be classified as deserters and their names removed from the unit's roster; that would sharply reduce the AWOL rate. I would want to get the necessary paperwork started as soon as possible. He agreed and offered to have the work done at battalion headquarters under supervision of his administrative warrant officer. I welcomed the offer of assistance but stated my preference to have the forms prepared in my orderly room. That way the word would quickly get out to the men, and one advantage I saw in having these longtime absentees declared deserters was to deter similar conduct in the future. He chuckled: "That's right, you *are* a lawyer!"

This was, however, not the only thing I did to overcome the AWOL problem. I talked it over with Sergeant Morrison and got the colonel's approval of my plan. The following Monday, instead of taking the reveille formation, I was, with two sergeants, riding a three-quarter-ton truck toward Morehead City. I stopped at the sheriff's office and inquired if any of my men had been arrested over the weekend. Indeed, seven of them were in the county jail awaiting hearing by the local magistrate later in the day. I posted bond for them and took them back to Fort Bragg with me. After we got back, I told them that they were restricted for two weeks and that this was the last time I would do this for them. The next time they would not only have to sit out their sentences in the county jail (and be listed as AWOL while they did) but would also receive the maximum punishment which I, as battery commander, could impose. (At the time that was thirty days' restriction and extra duties for the same period of time.) Only one of the men involved ever again gave me any trouble.

A few weeks later I found that, while the problem with men going home to Morehead City had virtually disappeared, some of them were now, with some regularity, getting into trouble on weekends in Fayetteville. I went into the city and talked with the county solicitor (the local prosecutor). He turned out to be a recent graduate of the Virginia law school, and he suggested that he would ask the judge to allow me to appear in court on behalf of any of my men who might have to respond to charges in his court.

I did not have to do this very often, and the judge was, I thought, quite fair to the malefactors from my battery. But I also got a rather dramatic demonstration of the ways of southern justice.

It must have been the second or third time that I found myself sitting in the rear of the courtroom, waiting for one of my men's cases to be called, that the bailiff called the case of Miss X. A young white woman, stylishly dressed, pearls around her neck and a mink stole draped over her arm, stepped forward. The judge actually rose to greet her and expressed his regret that she was again before him. She had promised that she would give no further cause for the police to have to bring her into court. The arresting officer testified that he had been called to the USO (the United Service Organizations provided off-duty recreational facilities for servicemen) where Miss X, dancing nude on a table, was the center of a large and unruly crowd. When asked by the judge, she explained that she had been at a party (she named the hosts, whom the judge evidently knew) and had afterward decided that she wanted to show the servicemen that, contrary to their belief, the young ladies of Fayetteville society were not snooty. She could not quite remember how she happened to disrobe and begin to dance, but then, she allowed, she had had quite a bit to drink at that party. The judge sighed: "You are really making this very difficult for me. With all the previous problems we have had with you, I should really give you a jail term. So this *really* has to be the last time, you understand that?" Miss X assured him, in the best southern drawl, that she was going to be good in the future. He fined her two hundred dollars. She promptly produced a sizeable roll of bills from her handbag and peeled off two. The judge again rose to bid her a good day.

The next case was that of a black woman who, so the arresting officer testified, had used profane language in public. The incident had taken place on the main thoroughfare of the city where "Maizie" (the judge never used her last name) had loudly berated the man with her. She explained that the man was her "no-good, lazy bum" of a husband. "You do your cussing at home," said the judge. "We can't have people running around cussing in public. That will be six weeks in the county farm." The bailiff escorted "Maizie" out of the room to begin her sentence. I was appalled at the contrast.

As Colonel Harriss had promised, three additional officers were soon assigned to the battery. This enabled me to spend most of my time going from section to section to observe training. Sergeant Morrison concentrated on the appearance of the barracks and the battery area. The executive officer, Jim Brooks, after a few minor initial problems, became a competent and reliable second-in-command. Al Graves, one of the two second lieutenants, brand-new out of OCS, did a superb job of getting the motor pool in shape, especially after I approved his recommendation to take one of the draftee privates and make him acting sergeant in charge of the motor section.[5]

I had problems with the other second lieutenant (whose name is immaterial here), a recent ROTC graduate from one of the state's leading universities. I had placed him in charge of the radar platoon and had made it very clear to him that the condition of the platoon barracks was a matter of concern. Two weeks later, at my Saturday inspection, the barracks was totally unsatisfactory. I directed that all personnel of the section remain on post and prepare for a reinspection, which I would carry out at 4:00 P.M. on Sunday.

I told the lieutenant that, as the platoon officer, it was his duty to supervise the men's efforts to improve the appearance of their barracks. Shortly afterward he came into my office to say that he could not do what I had asked: he had a social engagement that evening in the state capital. I observed that I had not *asked* him to stay on post, I had given him an order. He told me that I was unreasonable and inconsiderate, that he was entitled to have the weekend off, and that the plans he had for this particular weekend had been made before he had come to duty in Battery C.

The latter point, I told him, was totally irrelevant; in the army, you do not work from eight to five, you are on duty at all times unless specifically given time off. He replied that I evidently failed to realize that his family were important people in North Carolina and that he had social responsibilities that he could not cancel on short notice. I decided that I was not going to let this argument go on. I reached for a piece of official stationery, threaded it into my typewriter and pecked out a written order to him to remain on post, to be present in the barracks at specific hours, to perform a preliminary inspection at 1:00 P.M. on Sunday, and to be present for the reinspection I would perform.

He still did not seem to get the point. I reached for the *Manual of Court-Martial* and read him the section on disobeying a lawful order. He looked at me in total astonishment: "You wouldn't?" he said. I assured

5. Graves stayed in the army, and I saw him years later when, as a major, he attended the Command General Staff College at Fort Leavenworth.

him that, as far I was concerned, he had his orders from me, and, if he failed to carry them out, I would prefer charges against him. He turned to the door and let fly with an obscenity. I called him back and observed that that conduct, too, could become the subject of the charges I might bring. "Now," I said as calmly as I could, "you come to attention, give me a proper salute, do a smart about-face, and leave the room and close the door gently." I had finally gotten his attention. But he remained sullen and resentful, and eventually I asked Colonel Harriss to get him out of my battery (and the colonel concluded that he did not want him anywhere in his battalion). Just to complete the story: the young man's date that evening was the governor's daughter; the governor called the post commander, and that three-star general approved my action.

His replacement, a black officer by the name of Tuttle, then fit in very well with the kind of outfit I wanted C Battery to be. Fortunately Tuttle knew enough about the radar sets to make that section ready to perform its duties and do them well.

That things began to improve was at least partly due to Colonel Harriss's willingness to approve the designation of "acting Jacks" (who wore their corporal or sergeants' stripes not on their uniforms but on black armbands). When it had first been called into federal service, the 449th (just like the 758th) had received a large group of newly inducted draftees to bring it up to strength. The previous battalion commander had sought to protect his National Guard comrades and had, whenever possible, met the levies for shipment to Korea by sending out draftees. Now the levies were used to open the way for draftees with leadership potential and make them noncoms. It worked for Battery C, and it worked for the entire battalion.

Every time somebody was thus promoted I would make a little ceremony out of it, followed by taking the newly promoted soldier (and, if he was married, his wife) out to dinner in the city that weekend. The colonel allowed me to award three-day passes each month to a certain number of men who had performed especially well. The men began to take pride in what they were doing. After we were told that the next administrative inspection by Third Army would take place in May, I talked often about the importance of not just passing but being adjudged the best battery in the battalion.

By that time Donna had rejoined me at Fort Bragg. Once again we had found a sublease, this time the house of a major, who also left his car for us to use. This made it possible for us to take in an occasional evening meal at the officers' club and even once or twice a weekend trip to Raleigh. But her life was still rather lonely; I left the house every morning at 5:00 A.M. and often did not return until 7:00 or 8:00 at night. It did not surprise me when, after a few months, she suggested that she would like to join her mother on a trip to the West Coast.

But my efforts with the battery, so I wanted to think, paid off. We passed the administrative inspection with flying colors, best of the battalion's four batteries. The colonel allowed me to give the entire battery a day off. When the men came back from that extended weekend, a delegation came in to see me: What would they have to do to make sure that we did equally well on the training test? I went to battalion headquarters and got the colonel's permission to move the entire battery out on the artillery range for three days every week. (It helped that I remembered much of the layout from my basic training days almost ten years earlier.)

We ran every training exercise in the book and some that were not in the book. One of the things I had learned during my assignment with the Third Army testing team was that the team sometimes declared a piece of equipment out of operation and expected the unit to come up with makeshift substitutes. I built that into our training and challenged the men to come up with ideas. If an instrument operator had trouble working his piece of equipment, I or one of the other officers would take over, perform the requisite operation, and then, on the spot, instruct the man on the proper way to handle the equipment.

An observation battalion's function is to discover where the enemy's artillery is, in other words, to establish data for what the artillery calls counterbattery fire. There were only three such units in the army—one in Korea, one at the artillery school at Fort Sill, and the 449th. Each battalion had, in addition to a headquarters and service battery, three observation batteries, each with a survey platoon, a sound-ranging platoon (which employed sensitive microphones and electronic plotting equipment), a radar-ranging platoon, and the necessary support elements (motor pool, supply, mess, and orderly room). In a combat situation, such a battalion would cover the front of an entire corps and, typically, each battery, the sector of a division. This, of course, meant that the different elements were widely scattered and that the men had to be able to operate most of the time without the direct supervision of an officer. I conducted a competition between teams within each section, and the men responded well. We passed the training test with a score of ninety-five out of one hundred, well ahead of the other three batteries and of the battalion's overall score. I sent Sergeant Morrison into Fayetteville to make the necessary arrangements and treated the whole battery to a victory celebration. Battery C was riding high.

I took two weeks' leave in July, which Donna and I spent with my father and stepmother at the summer home they had recently acquired on Tanglewood Lake near New Milford, Connecticut. On my return, I found that Jim Brooks had, on his own initiative, prepared a list of things we might do to further our chances of winning the Third Army designation as the best company-sized unit. It was a good list, and we carried it out and with success. Early in October, the Third Army commander, Lieutenant General Edelman, came to Fort Bragg and, in the presence of all the brass of the post,[6] presented me with a large plaque that declared Battery C, 449th Field Artillery Observation Battalion, to be the best company-sized unit in the Third Army.

Colonel Harriss was immensely pleased. He invited me to lunch at the officers' club where he tried to convince me that I really ought to make the army my career. I told him that there had been a time when I had really intended to do that, and why I had changed my mind. He recited all the advantages of life in the Regular Army. By coincidence, I happened to have in my billfold the wallet-size form issued to me by the University of Kansas that attested to my appointment for the academic year 1952–1953 (as a tenured associate professor), and the salary I would be paid if I had not been on leave for military service. I showed it to the colonel: It was quite a bit more than my pay as a captain in the army. That effectively put an end to his sales talk.

A few weeks later, the army issued a directive that all reserve officers who had more than six years' total active duty were to be released. That, of course, applied to me. I turned the battery over to Jim Brooks and, shortly before Christmas 1952, left the army once again for the life of an academic.

6. To my pleasant surprise (and his) one of the generals in attendance was "Tommy" Lang, now the artillery commander of the Eighty-second Airborne Division but in World War II, of course, the executive officer of *my* Divarty.

Fort Leavenworth, Kansas

By the time I returned to Lawrence and my job at the University of Kansas I had spent over ten years in the United States Army, nearly two-thirds of that time on active duty. Under the law governing the reserve forces, a reservist could qualify for retirement with pay at the age of sixty; time spent on active duty was counted as such, but inactive duty was measured by a rather complicated point system that credited training days, completion of correspondence courses, and other factors at varying levels. In light of the credits I had already earned it made sense for me to remain in the reserve and eventually qualify for retired pay.

But there was a problem: the only reserve unit now in Lawrence was the headquarters of an infantry battalion and one of its rifle companies. I went with the unit to Fort Carson, Colorado, for summer camp that year but felt like a fish out of water. The clincher was the flat statement by the colonel commanding the reserve regiment that, not being an infantry officer, I could not expect to be further promoted.

I was about to write a letter to the Department of the Army requesting termination of my status as an officer in the active reserve, when I received, first, a phone call, then a letter from the army's Command and General Staff College at Fort Leavenworth offering me an interesting and advantageous alternative. The army had decided that the rather unplanned utilization of reserve officers with academic qualifications that the college could use (i.e., the type of duty that I had performed there in the summers of 1949 and 1950) did not yield the continuity its higher headquarters wanted at the college. What seemed preferable was that a number of reservists, perhaps a smaller group, should be identified as "mobilization designees" to the college; this would allow each individual to be slotted for a specific position which he would fill if the army found it necessary, especially in the case of more or less general mobilization, to draw away officers of the Regular Army from C&GSC to combat commands or higher staff assignments.

The letter went on to advise me that, if I accepted the mobilization designation, I would be assigned to understudy and work with the officer charged with the responsibility for the instruction on "Legal Problems of Command." C&GSC would pay from its own funds two weeks of active duty each summer, in addition to the two weeks paid from funds for the summer training of reserves, so I could expect to have a full month paid by the army each summer.

The original phone call had come from Dr. Ivan Birrer, the civilian educational adviser of C&GSC, and he now confirmed these arrangements and urged me to accept. Birrer and I had come to know each other during my earlier summer tours of duty at C&GSC, and he told me that he was particularly pleased to have me available as he continued his battle against the old army practice that every item of school instruction had to be presented in exactly the words approved by a review board. Through his daughter at KU he knew that I had already acquired a reputation as a good teacher and that I taught all my classes without the use of notes.

Birrer had been in his civilian job for eight or nine years by this time and previously had been through C&GSC's regular course, but he had not counted on the bureaucracy. When I checked in the following summer for my first tour of active duty as a mobilization designee, the colonel in charge of the section to which I had been assigned told me that, before I would be allowed to work on *anything* else, I had to complete a two-week course on methods of instruction. Birrer was flabbergasted but could not get an exception for me; not even the fact that I had actually *taught* such a course during my duty period in Japan made any difference.

By contrast, once I had demonstrated that I could handle a class, C&GSC was remarkably active in building my dossier for the future. They urged me to prepare and strongly supported an application for constructive credit for the basic course at the field artillery school and, once that had succeeded, for credit for the advanced course, based on my staff service at both the battalion and the division artillery level. Finally, after I had held my mobilization designation with them for ten years, they gave me credit for the regular year-long course at C&GSC itself. By that time I was a major and still had not attended any army school, at any level!

In about the third or fourth year of my service in this mobilization slot I was moved from the teaching department to which I had been assigned to become the understudy for the editor of the *Military Review*. *MR* had been started in the early thirties, mainly to provide a publication outlet for C&GSC faculty members; after World War II it opened its pages to a broader range of authors and also provided two parallel editions, Spanish and Portuguese, respectively. Its editor was now a full colonel, with a lieutenant colonel as deputy; the Spanish edition was overseen by an officer, always a recent graduate of C&GSC, from one of the Spanish American countries, the Portuguese edition by a similarly qualified officer from Brazil. A small group of civilian employees included two translators, one for each of the two foreign-language editions, typists, and a graphic artist who was also responsible for the journals' layout.

The arrangement was that I came on active duty for thirty days, the first two weeks to coincide with the second half of the deputy editor's annual leave and the second two weeks with the first two weeks of the editor's leave. In this month I was expected to prepare an entire issue (usually sixty-four pages) of *MR*. I found this interesting duty, and both the colonels I served under, Kenneth Lay and Don Delaney, became good friends, especially the latter. He remained in Leavenworth after he retired and sent his son to KU where he eventually earned a law degree and did sufficiently well that we actually tried a few years later, without success, to bring him back to join our faculty.

Early on I had concluded that commuting to Leavenworth on a daily basis (driving into the sun each way) was a rather trying chore; I made it a practice to request a room on the post where I stayed overnight from Monday through Friday. I usually carried some work with me from Lawrence as well as a Dictaphone and used my evenings to dictate letters and other writing. My small book *The Presidency: A Modern Perspective* (1960) came about in this manner.

I had reached the rank of major in 1957, and Ivan Birrer started talking about the next promotion. But when it came time to start on the necessary paperwork, it turned out that the army's office of career management (often disrespectfully referred to as "career mangle-ment") required that I submit, along with the promotion papers, an application for the year-long course of the Army War College (at Carlisle Barracks, Pennsylvania) or a similar strategy-oriented program. But this could not be done except by resident attendance for a full year. To do so would require that I take a year's leave without pay from the university and, given my status and salary at the university, I simply could not afford it.

But, without my knowledge everybody from the Army Chief of Staff on down got involved in my situation. The Chief of Staff at the time was Gen. Harold K. Johnson who, only a few years earlier, had been the commandant at Fort Leavenworth. Until he came to this post my contact with the commanding general had been limited to a matter of minutes on my second day of active duty when the officer I was working with (or for) would take me in to be introduced. Most of the time it was "in and out," usually without enough time to even be offered a chair, let alone a cup of coffee.

General Johnson was different. He asked me to sit down and tell him what I had done during World War II and during the Korean War, what kinds of courses I taught at the university, what my administrative responsibilities were there, how my family reacted to all the things I appeared to be involved in. He mentioned that Ivan Birrer had given him a copy of my book on the presidency and that he had read it.

As he rose to finish the interview, he said that he thought that Mrs. Johnson might like to meet me and that he might find an opportunity to arrange this.

I took these parting words to be the kind of polite statement people often make: "I'll give you a call and we'll have lunch," but a week later the general's secretary called and conveyed an invitation to, she said, an "informal" lunch the following week at General Johnson's residence. The occasion, she went on, was the visit to the college of Gen. William Westmoreland, then the commanding general in Vietnam, who was scheduled to make a presentation to the college community that morning.

Of course I accepted, but then I went into Colonel Lay's office (by this time my assignment had been changed from the teaching department to the *Military Review*) and asked him what was meant by the invitation being "informal." He laughed and said it was shorthand for telling me that I should wear whatever uniform I was wearing at work that day. Then he looked up and added that it might, however, be a good idea to wear a well- starched, clean shirt and, yes, all my ribbons.

That was good advice. General Westmoreland and his aide, a full colonel, were in green blouses, as was General Johnson and his aide. Roughly a dozen other officers, all colonels, were informal (tieless), but the shirts all looked tailor-made, and everybody wore ribbons. I noticed that, as we were being introduced to Westmoreland, the visitor looked each person in the face and then scanned the ribbons on his chest. General Johnson was evidently impressed that, as he was about to introduce me to John Anderson, the governor of Kansas, who stood next to Westmoreland in the receiving line, the governor anticipated the introduction and greeted me by my first name.

General Johnson's aide, the only major present besides myself, called my attention to the seating chart; I had been placed to Mrs. Johnson's left. After a few perfunctory exchanges, she surprised me by telling me why she had asked to have me seated next to her. "Harold," she said, "my husband, the general, cannot bring himself to talk about our son. But we need to have someone to give us a hand with him, before it is too late. Keith is bright, we know that. But he has been in rebellion against his father, and to a lesser degree also against me, ever since he entered high school. Now he has flunked out of two universities and has flatly told us that he had done so deliberately. He simply does not want to do anything his father and I have started for him. I have been talking to Dr. Birrer about the problem, and Ivan suggested that we (or at least I) talk to you while you are here." I did not know where this would lead, but she was so gracious and at the same time seemed so troubled that I asked if it would be appropriate for me to come back at some other time when she might tell me what she was expecting from me.[1]

That evening, as I talked to my wife on the phone, I shared this exchange with Mrs. Johnson with her. She sighed and commented on the frequency with which I was encountering bright young people who denied themselves the full opportunities the university offered, simply because they were in revolt against the parents who had insisted that

1. There is only one mention of Keith: the fact of his birth.

they go there. She reminded me of the young man from the small town in western Kansas who, by virtue of both his test scores and his high school grades, had been taken into the college honors program (which I then directed) but managed to accumulate a straight "F" record in his first semester in Lawrence. When I talked to him about it, he had displayed raw anger: his father had demanded that he get nothing but "A's" in high school; now he was getting even with him. He would not even file a petition for reinstatement; he was old enough to be able to enlist in a military service without parental consent, and he would complete the process that very day. Donna recalled how pleased I was when the same young man came back, after four years in the air force, and asked if he could start all over again. (He was still an undergraduate at the time we talked about him. But I am certain that eventually he earned a Ph.D. and became a well-known research scientist. Father and son reconciled after grandchildren appeared on the scene.)

Donna asked if I thought that I could come up with a solution for Keith Johnson that the son would not perceive as having originated with his father. Clearly, as with the boy from western Kansas, anything that bore the label "Dad's idea" was only going to arouse the son's resentment and add to the hostility. We talked at some length, and, as always, she steered me in the right direction. It required the assistance of the dean of students' office; I called Don Alderson, the dean of men, explained the situation, and, as I had rather expected, found him receptive to the approach I wanted to try.

When I called Mrs. Johnson the following day, she was eager that we talk the same day and asked me to come to the residence that afternoon. She was evidently tense but approached our conversation as if she had planned for it. Did I know the general's history? (It soon became clear to me that she hardly ever used his first name; it was always "the general.") I did. It was common knowledge that Harold Johnson, then a captain, had been taken prisoner on Bataan and had survived the infamous "death march" and the three years of captivity that followed. He made no secret of the importance he attributed to the religious faith that helped him in those years. That much I had heard; Mrs. Johnson added that "the general" had, in his youth and in his adulthood, admired Shakespeare; as a prisoner of war he would while away the time reciting the Bard's poetry and entire scenes from his plays. He also began to write poetry, something he still did.

Their reunion, so Mrs. Johnson confided, had been full of stress. The Japanese assumed that American soldiers who had been taken prisoners would, on their return home, be regarded as the Japanese did their own: permanently disgraced. They constantly berated their American prisoners, reminding them of their shame and the disgrace that they represented. The only news that reached the prisoners came from "Axis Sally," a part-American, part-Filipino woman who broadcast English-language propaganda on behalf of the Japanese; one of her recurring points was that, "of course," the wives the prisoners had left behind had by now married others or at least become other men's lovers. It had taken considerable time for the general to regain his inner strength. Having Keith with them was a major factor in helping them overcome that stressful time, which made it doubly difficult to cope with what Mrs. Johnson characterized as far more hostility than one could attribute to teenage revolt.

As a result of her tearful pleas, Mrs. Johnson related, Keith had come to Leavenworth with the family but had moved out after two weeks because he did not want to accept anything, "not even the roof over his head," from his father. He was now living at the YMCA, working full time at a hamburger stand (McDonald's had yet to come), and occasionally doing some babysitting, although the only family on the post that he would do this for was that of Dr. Birrer (a man who did not wear a uniform). That last bit of information was useful to me because part of my plan was to get to know Keith without parental intervention. I explained parts of my intentions to Mrs. Johnson and got her to agree to keep the information from her husband, especially since I assumed that, regardless of what I might say to him, he would want to be (or appear to be) the key player in the final act.

It all worked to perfection. I met Keith, seemingly by coincidence, at the Birrers' home. He accepted an invitation to come to Lawrence and stay with us over a weekend (that happened to involve a track meet that interested him); in the course of the weekend I got out of him that he really wanted to go to college, just not where his dad wanted him to go and without his dad holding the pocketbook whip over him. I explained my plan to him, and he lit up with pleasure: His mother would be relieved to see him in college *and* his father would be satisfied.

On my last day at C&GSC I made an appointment to pay my respects to the general. The prime purpose of my call was, of course, to set the stage for the resolution of his son's problem. I suggested that the general call the office of the College of Liberal Arts and Sciences at the university in about a week and make an appointment for himself and his son to see me. I told him that I had had an opportunity to talk to Keith and that the young man had agreed to come with his father and to bring along an application for admission, since on the record alone he was, of course, not admissible. The general seemed pleased although I mentioned that the decision would not be in my hands alone but would have to be reached by a committee. He grinned when I said that, knowing that I was at *the* place that prepared officers for duty on higher staffs, I did what a good staff officer would do: I handed him a map of the city of Lawrence and another showing details of the campus, both marked to show how he could best reach my office. As I left his office, his secretary (she had held that position under ten different commanders and knew just what she needed to do) asked if there was anything she needed to mark on the general's calendar; I told her that exactly a week later she should call the number I gave her and make an appointment for the general and his son (her eyebrow went up) to see me; I would have left instructions to make sure that the call was properly answered at the other end.

At the appointed time our office manager knocked at my office door and informed me that General Johnson was here, his son in tow. "Daddy has a chest full of fruit salad!" she added with a grin. Indeed, the general was fully decked out. Keith wore khaki slacks and a white shirt; if he had given in on the apparel, the quid pro quo obviously was that he had not gotten a haircut. It was somewhat incongruous to be addressed as "sir" by a two-star general, but I took it as a good sign.

I invited father and son into my office where (as I expected) the general proceeded to take charge of the meeting. He had prepared himself for the occasion and, although I had the impression that, more than once, his frustration with his son was going to erupt, he gave me a fairly calm account of Keith's educational misdeeds. Then, in the inflections of a military order, he told Keith to hand me the petition he had prepared.

I took my time reading the two handwritten pages. Then I suggested to the general that I needed to talk to his son alone. General Johnson bristled; I deliberately had not prepared him for this demand, because I needed, quite early, to establish that he was now on *my* turf and that we would play by *my* rules. So I remained adamant: I could not submit the petition to the committee without a private discussion with the main person involved, the student seeking admission. The general departed and took a seat in the outer office.

I asked Keith if he had given any thought to what he would want to study, assuming that the University of Kansas admitted him. (He had no transferable credits from either of the two universities where he had previously been enrolled.) To my surprise he told me that he had borrowed a catalog of the University of Kansas from Dr. Birrer's office and that he had noticed that one of the foreign languages one could major in was Chinese; did I think that made sense? I told him that only a few years earlier I had attempted the study of Chinese but had to give up after the first year because I simply could not find the time to spend with the sound tapes at the language laboratory. But I also mentioned that I had been steering some of our best students in the direction of the languages that few Americans ever studied and that I was convinced that even only a reading knowledge of Chinese would be sought after in years to come.

After about ten minutes of this conversation I told Keith that I would now take him to the office of Dean Alderson, the dean of men, and I would tell his father that I was taking him to meet with a subcommittee that would need to interview him, again without his father being present. This time the general did not even attempt to come along.

Don Alderson and I had worked together in a variety of contexts and had become good friends. He would die prematurely, but it is fitting that one of the largest auditoria on our campus bears his name. At the time of the event in question, he was dean of men and in that capacity had oversight of the university's large system of student residences. He was also a valuable member of the Liberal Arts College's reinstatement committee. The two of us had discussed the case of the general's son, but he had not yet met the young man.

After about fifteen minutes, in which Don examined Keith rather thoroughly, we told the young man to step out and wait for us in Don's outer office. Don confirmed that he was willing to follow my plan. We asked Keith to return and have a seat. As we had agreed, Don did the talking. We were, he told Keith, willing to take a chance on him. We understood how important it was for him to feel that he could live free of the close control of his father, and we had a way in which this could be done. Acting as a subcommittee of the reinstatement committee, we would authorize the admissions office to allow him to enter the University of Kansas *but* on the condition that he live in a university-owned living facility, specifically McCollum Hall (which housed over nine hundred students). I told him that, when we now returned to my office, I would inform his father that the committee had voted to admit him but with the condition that he live in one of the residence halls. The remainder of our arrangement we would regard as a private conversation between the three of us: If he proved himself in the residence hall, he would, after sixty days, be appointed a residence hall assistant, with a stipend that would allow him to continue in school without financial support from his family. Keith was so flabbergasted that he asked us to repeat what we had said. This time I added: "And if you let us down, there will be no second chance here nor probably anyplace else."

General Johnson beamed when I apprised him of the outcome. Twice during the next year, my wife and I were invited for dinner at the commandant's house at Fort Leavenworth. Then the general was transferred to the general staff in Washington where, in short order, he jumped a number of his seniors to become the Army Chief of Staff.

Apparently he felt that it behooved him now to see that good things happened to me in the army. Ivan Birrer told me later that General Johnson had called several times to inquire if there was anything he could or should do to help with my advancement in rank. Birrer told me that on one occasion the Chief of Staff had four other generals in his office to figure out what could be done for Major Heller. But the personnel managers adamantly insisted that I had already been allowed to move up in rank too far without meeting the formal schooling requirements. General Johnson told me, in the course of a proud visit to see Keith receive not his first degree at KU but his master's degree in Chinese language and literature, that the vice chief of staff had wondered out loud and only half in jest whether he, Johnson, was planning to bring me all the way to a general's star without any but constructive military school credits. But by that time I had already concluded that I had probably gotten as far in the army, short of being a Regular Army officer, as I would ever get.

I had been able to help the Command and General Staff College to receive approval not only to offer graduate work but to award the master's degree to its top graduates. Then, for two terms of three years each I served on the Civilian Educator's Advisory Committee to C&GSC. That ended in 1975, severing my last formal tie to Fort Leavenworth and the C&GSC, but for years afterward I would hear from people I had worked with at the college. When I was asked to give a talk to the Leavenworth bar association in the early eighties, there were three gray-haired ladies in the front row who had been clerks at the *Military Review* when I worked there. When my wife died in 1990, not only Ivan Birrer but about a dozen others from Fort Leavenworth, including Colonels Lay and Delaney, attended the memorial service. There was a floral tribute from Mrs. Johnson (a widow by this time), and Keith came all the way from Washington (where he was gainfully and satisfyingly employed) to give me a hug.

Epilogue

Serendipity or Good Fortune

In the few weeks I spent with my parents in Warsaw in 1938, after I had left Vienna and before my ship would depart from Gdynia for New York, I tried to learn what I could about the United States. My father had purchased the then-new edition of James Bryce's *American Commonwealth* while in America in 1923. (The work was first published in 1888 and has been revised and reprinted many times since. Bryce, a Scotsman and scholar, served as the British ambassador to the United States from 1907 to 1913.) I do not know whether or when he had read it, but it was there for me to read in 1938. I remember that this was not easy; my knowledge of English was minimal. But my father allowed me to take the two volumes with me, sort of a beginning for my own library.

Reading it was difficult but became easier each time. As I returned to student life I mentioned to my intended dissertation supervisor that it was time for me to expand my perspective of early American history; to begin he urged Alexis de Tocqueville's *Democracy in America* (first English edition 1835 and 1840, with multiple later editions and numerous translations). I have read the work in several translations, as edited by different writers. Each time I have discovered new gems, new insights, new invitations to reflect.

One instance is Tocqueville's observation that Americans are, by nature, joiners. I had not had much time to notice that myself. In law school (sometimes working four different jobs to keep body and soul together) I found that time was always lacking. Accounts of soldiers' lives tend to leave the impression that they are mostly waiting, interrupted by bursts of hectic, sometimes violent, activity. That was not the way it was for me; learning various jobs was almost continuous and, while the moments of activity may not have been continuous, they consumed time and effort. It was easier to find time for reading as an academic.

Even so I found little time for idle immersions of various kinds. I agreed to spend time on committees (city planning committee, governor's committee on constitutional revision, dean's review of the university library, archbishop's planning board for services for students), accept books for review and write my own, plan and help direct for programs of academic advancement (honors program, international programs, etc.) Tocqueville may have had a different impression, but all I could do when I was asked to join was to decline.

What I had learned in the military was efficient performance on duty only invited added duties. That seemed to hold true in the academic world as well. By the mid-fifties I had acquired (probably not earned) a reputation as the university's champion member of committees. Actually my involvement with former president Harry Truman may have been the peak of multiple activities.

It started with a telephone call from the chancellor of the university, Dr. Franklin D. Murphy. Rather abruptly he asked what plans I had for the summer. Now summer school teaching was a sore subject with the KU faculty in those days. It was considered essential, but the state legislature had not seen fit to provide the necessary funds. This meant that the administration was reluctant to approve any courses to be taught that would not draw a substantial number of students (i.e., most courses were of the introductory variety) and that regardless of what one's nine-months salary was, there was a cap on summer school pay. Fortunately I had come to know Franklin Murphy in my early months at the university and did not think that he would misunderstand my reply: "Like most of your faculty, sir, I shall starve!"

Murphy said he was not joking: Would I be interested in working for former president Truman? "Doing what?" I asked. "I am not sure," Murphy replied. "It has something to do with the writing of his memoirs." I could not figure what this might mean but indicated my interest. Murphy told me to bring copies of my (then three) published books to his office, along with a curriculum vitae. I did as I was told.

About three weeks later two men associated with Mr. Truman came to Lawrence to interview me. One of them was William Hillman, a former journalist who, within the first two minutes, informed me that he had been the newspaperman who had first reported on King Edward VIII's affair with Mrs. Wallis Simpson, the affair that led to the resignation of the King. He led off, impressing on me how important the memoirs of a former president of the United States would be, especially in view of the fact that the last president to pen an autobiography had been William Howard Taft.[1] His colleague, David Noyes, a public relations man who had come to know Senator Truman in the days of World War II, could hardly wait for his turn, during which he offered an uninhibited paean to Harry S. Truman, "the Lincoln of the twentieth century," he called him.

I had no opportunity to ask questions. Hillman rose, said that, of course, the decision was up to the president, and bade me farewell. Noyes hugged me and repeated what he had said before, that I would be most fortunate if I were selected for "the job." Nobody had asked what I thought of President Truman or whether I had even voted for him in 1948. There was no mention of any pay that might attach to the task. I told my wife that we might still spend the summer without income.

But about another three weeks later there came a call from Miss Rose Conway, who identified herself as President Truman's secretary and asked if I could come to Kansas City the following day to meet with Mr. Truman. It was, she said, about "the job." She instructed me on where I was to go and urged me to be on time, because, she said, the former president had a very busy schedule. I could not figure what might keep him so busy but made certain to be punctual.

In those days there was no provision at all for former chief executives: no retirement pay, no office space, no clerical help, no free-mail privilege, no Secret Service protection. Mr. Truman had rented office space in the Federal Reserve bank building in downtown Kansas City, Missouri, five rooms on the eleventh floor (with a larger storage area on the floor

1. I did not interpose that he was wrong, that there existed a published *Autobiography of Calvin Coolidge* (New York: Cosmopolitan, 1929) and that Herbert Hoover had written several volumes of an autobiographical nature.

below). It was to the eleventh-floor office that I went at the appointed hour and entered a door simply labeled "Harry S Truman."

It was a small, unadorned entry area with a bank of file cabinets on one side and a few plain chairs for visitors on the other. I walked up to the receptionist and gave her my name. At that the man who was bent over one of the files turned around and held out his hand: "I am Harry Truman. Come into my office." He introduced me to the woman at the desk, Frances Williams, then ushered me into a larger, but equally plain room where I met Rose Conway. From her office an opening led into a smaller room where a man was squatting on the floor, busily engaged in sorting three-by-five cards spread out over the linoleum. Mr. Truman introduced me to Dr. Morton Royce who, he said, had been helping him. He did not care, apparently, to have me get to know Dr. Royce, which was understandable, since he was the man I would replace.

From there the former president led me into his office, the only room in the suite that had any kind of decor. Most of the items, I later learned, were gifts that had come to him while he was in office, and he expected to turn those over to the library which would be the depository of his papers. He asked me to sit across the desk from him; my three books were plainly visible. He said he had looked into all of them. The one he liked best, he said, was the account of what had happened to the Virginia state government during World War II; it did not have any lawyer talk, he opined.

Then he asked me how I would go about doing "the job," still leaving me in the dark about the specifics of it. Earlier in the day, on the hour's drive into Kansas City, I had recalled how indefinite Hillman and Noyes had been about the work I was expected to do. Suppose Mr. Truman asked me what *my* perception was? I had come up with what I thought might be an answer if Mr. Truman were to ask me that question. Thus prepared, I now told him that I would approach the task (being as indefinite about it as he had been) in the same way I had learned to function as a staff officer in the military. I would pay close attention to what the commander wanted and implement those desires to meet the commander's expectations.

That reply seemed to satisfy him, but it also opened up another avenue for conversation: military experiences. He confirmed that he had seen on my vita that I had served in both World War II and the Korean War and wanted to know what I had done during the latter. I explained that my active-duty period in 1951 and 1952 had really consisted of two quite different parts: first, getting a unit ready to be equipped with the atomic cannon; second, bringing a badly unprepared unit up to par.

What kind of guns did we have in that second unit? he asked. I told him that we had no guns at all, that the unit was a field artillery "observation" battalion. This was a new one for him (in fact, in both world wars, trial units had only been pieced together near the end of fighting in the European theater). He asked me to explain what an artillery observation battalion would do.

I asked if I might use a large piece of posterboard that I had spotted on a table along the wall. He agreed, and I diagramed the various ways in which an observation unit could locate where enemy artillery fire was coming from. Mr. Truman asked questions that indicated that he had not forgotten basic principles of artillery. It was clear that we had established a common bond.

This became more evident as I became more familiar with the former president's background. His military experience was clearly a watershed point in his life. Biographers have been hard put to explain Harry Truman on the basis of his early years. To me it became clear that his brief period as a combat commander in the Great War had changed his perspective: It had taught him that men would follow him when he challenged them to do so, and it had also taught him how important it is for a leader to act that role, to make it clear that he knows where to go and what to do.[2] I could understand that, as I believe that much the same happened to me, but, like Truman, I would be hard put to say when it happened and how.

It was good fortune, I would guess, that brought me to President Truman. Certainly it was good fortune and nothing I did that brought me to Jimmy Lester's attention. The confidence he displayed toward me after our night together at Tanamerah Bay translated itself into respect from the men I served with. When Carmel Wallace went back to the States on leave and I was named operations sergeant, nobody belittled my rapid promotion; the first sergeant did not even ask me before having my cot and my few belongings moved into his tent; that had become my due.

2. I made this point in my contribution on President Truman in Lord Longford and Sir John W. Wheeler-Bennett, eds., *The History Makers: Leaders and Statesmen of the 20th Century* (London: Sidgwick & Jackson, 1973), 32–35, 329.

I do not know that the thought entered my mind when I offered to go into the interior on the ambush assignment, but I know that I realized afterward that what happened to me on this assignment established for most of my cohorts that I was not merely a desk soldier. The unlikely friendship with Steve Targozinski stemmed from that episode.

I have already related how, at every step thereafter when I was likely to go into harm's way, Targo came forward to be at my side. But there is a sequel. Beginning in 1960 I found myself going to New York once or twice a month to attend various meetings that I had become involved in as a result of duties I had been given at the university. On one of the early trips I was standing outside LaGuardia Airport looking for a taxi when I heard my name called. As I turned toward the sound I saw Targozinski running toward me: if I wanted a taxi, he wanted me to ride in *his* cab. Before we reached my destination I had to promise that I would let him know whenever I was coming to New York so he could be at the airport to meet me, and there would be none of this nonsense about paying a fare. That arrangement continued until one day when Targo was not there. In his place was a young man who was obviously his son (Francis Targozinski, no less), and he brought me the sad news that his father had died suddenly of a brain aneurysm. He insisted on driving me into the city, at no charge, of course.

But the question of serendipity *versus* good fortune also arises in nonmilitary contexts. Once Donna had come to enjoy foreign travel we started to subscribe to travel magazines, with *Travel and Leisure*, published by the American Express company, becoming our favorite. The fall 1984 issue carried an intriguing essay describing narrow-gauge railroads in Austria. We were scheduled to spend the spring semester there. We took the magazine with us, planning to eventually take two of the narrow-gauge rail trips it described.

The first took us from St. Pölten, about thirty-five miles west of Vienna, to Mariazell, the foremost pilgrimage target in Austria, remote and high up in the Alps. The article had recommended a small hotel with nice rooms and a first-rate restaurant. What it did not tell us was that during the week it was virtually empty, and the owner's son, a baron, did all the work, especially the cooking (and it was superb). Since the dining room was vacant the count (whose English was very good) simply set a table for three in our suite and joined us. Thus we were able to get the answer to a puzzle along the rail line.

The train stopped frequently, allowing passengers (mostly of school age) to get on or off the train. Two of the stops had full-scale stations, but each of the others had only a small shelter that carried two signs: one, the place name, was obvious, but the other, just the two letters UH, was puzzling. The baron enlightened us. These shelters were stopping points, in German *Haltestelle,* and they were unattended, or *unbesetzt.* UH means unattended stopping point. We adopted that for our home calendar: UH equals an appointment that it is not necessary to keep. Serendipity or good fortune?

Our second narrow-gauge trip took us southwest from St. Pölten to the small town of Marbach and, more specifically, Castle Ernegg. Our reference article praised Ernegg for having retained old furnishings and old decor and serving excellent food for about forty guests. Nearby was a nine-hole golf course (which did not interest us but suggested that Ernegg might attract tourists from the British Isles).

The trip itself was quite pleasant, notable by the absence of UH signs. But at Marbach there might as well have been such a sign; there was no evidence of any kind of humanity. Only some exploration of the neighborhood unearthed the station master, who denied responsibility for getting us to the castle. Eventually another neighbor agreed to call and get a message to the castle (which was on the other side of the river, requiring a two-mile tour to a useable bridge).

The man who showed up with a horse-drawn carriage about a half hour later was full of explanations! This was all the fault of the countess, but the countess does not make any errors. The countess would meet us at the door to the castle, and he just knew that she was embarrassed because he had overheard her tell the cook to hold dessert until these delayed guests could join the assembled guests (English they were).

As we approached the castle we noticed a water-filled moat and the wooden bridge that had to be crossed to come to the castle. The gate was open, and inside stood a woman. She looked to be about forty, dressed in what people would call a *Prachtolirndl* (a luxury rural dress), heavily jeweled and a crown of flowers on her head. She said, "Welcome to Schloss Ernegg," first in German and then in English. As our carriage came to a halt she stepped up to it and, in good English, called out: "I am so sorry about your inconvenience. I am Elsbeth and I am glad that you are here. Josef (our coachman) will carry your suitcases. Let me show you your room." Her smile was truly welcoming.

We were taken to an indoor gate and up a flight of stairs. Our room was spacious, rather elegantly furnished, with a washstand on one side, a table with four chairs on the other, and across the room from the entrance was a french door leading to a balcony. Elsbeth told us that we shared a bathroom with four other guests whose rooms adjoined ours. She suggested that we use it and then she would escort us to the dining room.

On the way she explained that, while the castle could accommodate forty guests, our coming brought the number to thirty-eight, including an English tour director, two German (but English-speaking) drivers of their traveling coaches, and thirty-three teachers, mostly from Manchester. The kitchen staff, except for the Viennese chef, were all local but mostly spoke English. A white-jacketed waiter outside a door labeled "dining room" pulled a string to a bell. As the door opened we could see that everyone at the tables had risen.

Elsbeth called out, in English: "Ladies and Gentlemen! Professor and Mrs. Francis Heller, from the University of Kansas, U.S.A. They will be with us for three days. They have not eaten this evening. Thank you for waiting for them. Dessert and coffee will now be served." There was a round of applause as she guided us to a table where two places awaited us, each with a plate of cold cuts and fruit. We met the four other people at the table who cheerfully engaged us in conversation.

After dinner Elsbeth took us back to our room, which in the interval had been enriched by a large vase of fresh flowers and a tray with a bottle of champagne and three glasses. The refreshment, she explained was for our having to wait at the station, and she opened the bottle and joined us in enjoying the (high-quality) bubbly.

Over the drinks she introduced herself and gave us her story. Her name was Countess Auersperg. "Of the *palais*[3] in Vienna?" I asked. "Yes," she replied, "I owned that, too; I inherited both from my grandfather." "Who was Emperor Franz Josef's minister of agriculture," I noted. She wondered how I knew this; I explained that, although the emperor had died a year before I was born, I had had my early schooling in Vienna.

That triggered her account. Yes, her grandfather had been the minister,

3. Homes built in Vienna by the nobility were (and some still are) called by this French word.

but, by contrast to me, she had been born in England, as had her mother. Her family had had ties to England since the nineteenth century, and the minister's children had been educated in England while living with English relatives. That was where they were when the Great War started, and they were allowed to remain until the early twenties when they took up residence in Ernegg. There was not enough money to refurbish the place in Vienna (and I remembered that it stood empty in the twenties and was later used by what modern historians called Austro-Fascists, the followers of Dollfuss and Schuschnigg).

Elsbeth picked up the thread. Seeing the political turmoil in Austria and the growing strength of Hitler and his followers, her family thought it best to take their two teenage daughters to England to live and go to school. So another generation was spared being treated as enemy aliens. Instead both girls eventually married Englishmen. Elsbeth, born in 1947, was the child of such a union.

Ernegg (and Marbach) was in the part of Austria occupied by the Soviet Union. But Elsbeth's mother had come into some money, and the Austrian government contributed to the repair of the former family residence in Vienna. But Elsbeth (and her sister) followed the pattern of her mother's generation: go live with the relatives in England, go to school there, marry an Englishman, divorce him, wind up with a substantial alimony. Her husband was a sportsman who saw to it that Ernegg would have a golf course and shooting ranges for deer. Converting Ernegg into a tourist destination had been Elsbeth's idea.

Ernegg was restful for us. Elsbeth enjoyed our company and spent much time showing us the parts of the castle that she had made into a museum with souvenirs of earlier centuries. She loved to talk about her ancestors (which was one reason she had reclaimed the name Auersperg after her divorce).

There was an old fireplace in the section she called the museum. On the mantel was one line of a poem:

> Dürft' ich wohl so frei sein, frei zu sein

The poet's name was given as Anastasius Grün. I knew that the name was a cover, a pseudonym used by Count Anton Auersperg whose name appeared on early rosters of my (and his) Benedictine school in Vienna.

It astounded Elsbeth. It did not astonish Donna.
And the countess smiled. . . .

Serendipity or good fortune? In a book on Vienna (under that title)[4] that line from the poem is translated: "May I make so free as to be free?" Is the answer here the same as my memory? I leave it to the reader.

4. Translated by Ilsa Barca and published by Alfred A. Knopf in 1966, 167.

INDEX